3D ED

MARKETING
MATH

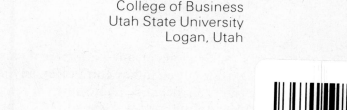

WILLIAM A. STULL

Professor of Business/
Marketing Education
College of Business
Utah State University
Logan, Utah

SB27CB
PUBLISHED BY
SOUTH-WESTERN PUBLISHING CO.
CINCINNATI, OH   DALLAS, TX   LIVERMORE, CA

ISBN: 0-538-60448-4

Library of Congress Catalog Card
Number: 89-61402

3 4 5 6 7 B 6 5 4 3 2

Printed in the United States of America

CONTENTS

TO THE STUDENT

The application of math skills is vital to solving marketing problems. This text-workbook is designed to help you develop the fundamental math skills required for successful careers in this important field. In this text-workbook, math used in marketing is presented in a logical sequence, from the time merchandise is ordered and received until it is sold. After successfully completing this text-workbook, you will be able to clearly see the importance of math in a marketing environment. You will also be able to see the corresponding effect of this cycle on the profitability of businesses.

Marketing Math is a self-contained unit of instruction that you may work on individually, in a small group, or with your entire class. This text-workbook is also designed to allow you to progress at your own learning pace, with the teacher serving as manager of this learning experience.

SECTION ORGANIZATION

Each of the six sections contained in this text-workbook begins with a series of clearly stated objectives that you are expected to accomplish. These objectives have been reviewed by persons employed in marketing to assure that they are needed by the entering worker. This list of objectives is followed by a short narrative relating to the first objective, a sample problem and solution (when necessary), and a learning activity in which you are asked to solve a typical marketing math problem. This procedure is followed for each objective stated. At the completion of each section, application problems and two job-oriented projects are provided.

OVERVIEW OF SECTIONS

Section 1. Basic Math Skill Review is designed to help those of you who may have weaknesses or difficulties in basic math by giving you a chance to improve or upgrade your skills in the areas of addition, subtraction, multiplication, division, decimals, fractions, and percentages. An unsatisfactory score on any part of the Self-Check (six parts) indicates that you should complete that basic math skill review found in Section 1.

Section 2. Ordering and Receiving Merchandise exposes you to the basic math involved with ordering, receiving, and recording incoming merchandise. Included in this section are the different types of discounts offered by manufacturers or distributors.

Section 3. Pricing Merchandise explains the importance of proper pricing and the methods used in pricing merchandise. You are shown how to use basic markup formulas, calculate markdowns on merchandise, determine unit selling prices, calculate prices for fractional quantities, and calculate the break-even point used in pricing products.

Section 4. Completing Daily Calculations in Marketing features the calculations involved in many of the activities required for a business to sell merchandise or services to customers. Topics included are: opening the cash register and verifying the accuracy of the opening change fund, completing cash and charge sales, making change properly, cashing checks, and proving the cash drawer at the end of the business day.

Section 5. Understanding Inventory Procedures explains the need for maintaining inventory records, which are critical to the success of a business. You learn about the different aspects of taking inventory as well as how selected inventory information is used by a business. From inventory information, you are introduced to a method for calculating the stock turnover rate and open to buy.

Section 6. Calculating Income and Loss in Marketing gives you an overview of how to determine the net income or loss for both service and merchandising businesses. In this section you will also learn how to construct an income statement for a merchandising business.

SUGGESTIONS

The introductory part of each section provides the rationale for the math calculations given. Following the narrative, a sample problem is provided so you can see how a typical problem of this type is solved. If you have difficulty in either the Learning Activity exercises or Using Math in Marketing application problems, simply turn back in the text and review how this type of problem is solved. Before beginning Section 1, be sure to complete the Basic Math Self-Check. If you have difficulty with any of the basic math skills, you can review and update those skills by completing Section 1.

The math skills you develop while completing this text-workbook will be very valuable to you as you progress in your marketing career. Whether or not you use electronic calculators as you complete this text-workbook is up to your classroom teacher. While calculators of all types can be found nearly everywhere today, there are times when a calculator may not be available and the marketing person must do the necessary math calculations manually. It is *not* recommended that you use electronic calculators to complete the Self-Check or Section 1. You should be able to complete these calculations manually. The use of calculators for Sections 2-6 is optional. Be sure, however, to check with your classroom teacher.

INSTRUCTIONS FOR BASIC MATH SELF-CHECK

Many marketing employers require job applicants to complete a basic math employment test before they can be employed. The Basic Math Self-Check is designed to help *you* identify any weaknesses you may have in basic math skills. The math calculations required for the *Marketing Math* problems will be much easier if your basic math skills are good.

Your score on the Basic Math Self-Check will indicate what parts, if any, of Section 1 of *Marketing Math* you should study before you begin

Section 2. A score of 80 percent or more on each part of the Self-Check indicates your skill in that area of basic math is adequate. A score of less than 80 percent on any part indicates a need for extra review. You should then complete the parts of Section 1 indicated by your Self-Check scores.

Each part of the Self-Check is timed. (Be sure you are timed when you work each part.) Do the entire Self-Check before beginning any section of *Marketing Math*. There are six separate parts to this Basic Math Self-Check.

Self-Check Part	Section 1 Coverage	Using Math in Marketing Problems at End of Section 1
Part I — Addition	pages 2-8	Problem 1, a-j, page 39
Part II — Subtraction	pages 8-13	Problem 2, a-j, page 40
Part III — Multiplication	pages 13-19	Problem 3, a-j, pages 40-41
Part IV — Division	pages 19-28	Problem 4, a-j, pages 41-42
Part V — Fractions	pages 28-35	Problem 5, a-n, p, pages 42-43
Part VI — Percents	pages 35-38	Problem 5, o, q, page 43

SECTION 1
BASIC MATH SKILL REVIEW

Can you add and subtract numbers rapidly and accurately? How good are you at multiplication and division? People employed in marketing jobs use these math skills every working day. Your success in understanding and solving the problems in this text-workbook depends on the basic math skills you develop and sharpen in this section.

Before proceeding any further, you should complete the basic math self-check that begins on page vii. When you have finished the self-check, you will be able to see which of the following basic math skills you should review and study in this section.

---

1. Adding correctly, saving time, and proving your answer.

2. Subtracting correctly and proving your answer.

3. Multiplying correctly and proving your answer.

4. Dividing correctly and proving your answer.

5. Adding, subtracting, multiplying, and dividing fractions.

6. Using percentages.

ADDING CORRECTLY

Illus. 1-1

Adding purchases while grocery shopping—either with or without a calculator—is a skill people use every day.

Basic Combinations in Addition

Basic addition skill is combining two numbers into one as quickly and accurately as possible. Did you know that forty-five addition combinations can be made using the numbers 1, 2, 3, 4, 5, 6, 7, 8, and 9?

Examine the 45 addition combinations below. Practice these combinations mentally to increase your speed and accuracy in addition.

5	4	4	2	7	2	2	3	9
+ 2	+ 7	+ 3	+ 2	+ 9	+ 1	+ 3	+ 5	+ 9
7	11	7	4	16	3	5	8	18

3	6	4	4	4	1	4	6	7
+ 8	+ 9	+ 9	+ 4	+ 2	+ 3	+ 1	+ 7	+ 3
11	15	13	8	6	4	5	13	10

5	5	1	2	6	5	7	1	4
+ 5	+ 9	+ 5	+ 6	+ 8	+ 6	+ 8	+ 6	+ 5
10	14	6	8	14	11	15	7	9

3	5	1	1	2	6	5	8	1
+ 9	+ 7	+ 1	+ 7	+ 8	+ 3	+ 8	+ 8	+ 8
12	12	2	8	10	9	13	16	9

2	2	7	8	1	3	4	6	4
+ 9	+ 7	+ 7	+ 9	+ 9	+ 3	+ 6	+ 6	+ 8
11	9	14	17	10	6	10	12	12

Add the following.

5 + 2	3 + 9	1 + 8	8 + 6	6 + 7
7 + 4	2 + 1	7 + 7	6 + 6	5 + 4
9 + 5	9 + 7	7 + 8	9 + 4	4 + 3
8 + 3	1 + 1	6 + 2	1 + 7	8 + 9
1 + 9	8 + 2	5 + 1	4 + 2	2 + 2
6 + 3	1 + 3	5 + 6	4 + 4	3 + 3
6 + 4	5 + 8	5 + 7	4 + 1	3 + 2
5 + 3	5 + 5	1 + 6	8 + 8	9 + 6
9 + 9	9 + 2	2 + 7	7 + 3	8 + 4

Combinations that Total 10

You can sharpen your addition skills if you can recognize the combinations of two and three numbers that total 10. Study the following combinations of two and three numbers that total 10.

Combinations of two numbers that total 10	5 5 ‾ 10	6 4 ‾ 10	7 3 ‾ 10	8 2 ‾ 10	9 1 ‾ 10		

Combinations of three numbers that total 10	8 1 1 ‾ 10	7 2 1 ‾ 10	6 3 1 ‾ 10	5 4 1 ‾ 10	6 2 2 ‾ 10	5 3 2 ‾ 10	4 3 3 ‾ 10	4 4 2 ‾ 10

2
Learning Activity

Circle the combinations of two and three numbers that total 10.

2 8 ‾	3 6 ‾	4 7 ‾	5 5 ‾	3 8 ‾	7 3 ‾	5 3 ‾	8 4 ‾	6 4 ‾	6 6 ‾

7 2 1 ‾	8 1 1 ‾	6 3 3 ‾	2 7 1 ‾	3 6 1 ‾	2 4 3 ‾	5 4 1 ‾	6 4 3 ‾	4 5 3 ‾	6 2 2 ‾

Adding by Combinations

One way to improve your skill in adding a column of numbers is to look for numbers that total 10. Look at the following example to understand this idea.

Example

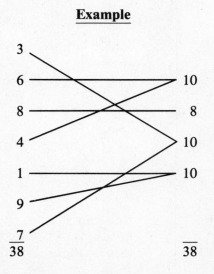

3
Learning Activity

Add the following columns of numbers using the combination approach just shown.

9	9	7	8	8
6	1	3	9	1
4	3	4	6	9
7	4	6	3	2
5	6	5	7	3
8	7	5	4	5
2	7	6	1	5

The combination approach can also be used by combining numbers into pairs. The following examples show how this is done.

Example 1

$$
\begin{array}{l}
4 \\
5
\end{array} \Big> 9 \\
\begin{array}{l}
7 \\
6
\end{array} \Big> 13 \Big> 22 \\
\begin{array}{l}
1 \\
3
\end{array} \Big> 4 \\
\begin{array}{l}
6 \\
8
\end{array} \Big> 14 \Big> 18 \\
\overline{40} \quad \overline{40} \quad \overline{40}
$$

Example 2

$$
\begin{array}{l}
6 \\
2
\end{array} \Big> 8 \\
\begin{array}{l}
3 \\
5
\end{array} \Big> 8 \\
\begin{array}{l}
1 \\
6
\end{array} \Big> 7 \\
\begin{array}{l}
3 \\
4
\end{array} \Big> 7 \\
\overline{30} \quad \overline{30}
$$

4
Learning Activity

Add the following columns using pairs of numbers in the combination approach.

6			9		
8			7		
3			5		
6			8		
4			6		
3	—	—	3	—	—

Adding Numbers with more than One Digit

When adding numbers with more than one digit, it is often necessary to carry over numbers to the next column on the left. The number carried should be written lightly over the left column so that it is not forgotten. Look at the two examples below.

<u>**Example 1**</u>

$$\begin{array}{r} {\scriptstyle 1} \\ 25 \\ +\ 9 \\ \hline 34 \end{array}$$

<u>**Example 2**</u>

$$\begin{array}{r} {\scriptstyle 1} \\ 25 \\ +\ 29 \\ \hline 54 \end{array}$$

5
Learning Activity

Add the following. Make sure you carry over the correct number.

15 + 8	24 + 9	13 + 7	18 + 5	27 + 6	12 + 9
14 + 7	16 + 4	19 + 3	21 + 9	23 + 8	17 + 4
24 + 7	68 + 5	25 + 5	29 + 5	31 + 9	32 + 9
38 + 4	35 + 8	58 + 2	46 + 8	49 + 7	27 + 5
95 + 9	37 + 4	38 + 4	97 + 6	89 + 23	88 + 23
57 + 9	49 + 87	97 + 65	87 + 49	84 + 47	84 + 47
78 + 54	69 + 23	67 + 13	39 + 25	33 + 29	58 + 46
44 + 38	57 + 84	47 + 68	34 + 28	68 + 47	64 + 28

Proving Your Answer in Addition

There are two methods of proving your answers in addition. The simplest is to add the column of numbers a second time in the opposite direction (Example 1). Another method (Example 2) is to add each column separately; then add those sums together. However, be sure to place each sum one digit to the left of the preceding sum, as shown in Example 2.

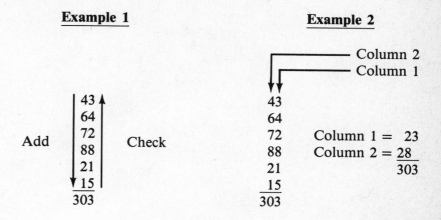

Example 1

Add | 43 ↑ 64 72 88 21 15 | Check
303

Example 2

Column 2
Column 1

43
64
72   Column 1 =   23
88   Column 2 = 28
21   303
15
303

6
Learning Activity

Add the following column of numbers and prove your answers.

Add | 17 ↑ 38 45 67 18 20 | Check

28
39
46
15
18
26

Column 1 = ___ ___

Column 2 = ___ ___

Adding Decimals

When adding numbers with decimal points, always place the decimal points directly under one another. Also, place the decimal point in the answer directly under the other decimal points in the problem.

$ 1.59
0.06
15.88
0.65
0.13   Decimal points are placed
$18.31   under one another.

Add the following columns of numbers. Rewrite any problems that are written incorrectly. Place the decimal point in the correct position in each answer.

$17.95	$39.50	21.50
6.50	1.29	3.98
0.79	3.65	0.9934
1.25	0.98	1.89
21.25	12.79	7.69

$16.00	216.735	$31.95
3.57	9.98	22.50
0.69	8.95	1.335
0.39	0.69	49.99
1.76	0.4949	29.95

SUBTRACTING CORRECTLY

Illus. 1-2

A salesperson uses subtraction to find the amount to be financed after a down payment.

Basic Subtraction Combinations

Subtracting accurately is another important skill used on a daily basis. Just as you learned in addition, there are also 45 combinations of one-digit numbers in subtraction. Study the answers to the subtraction combinations that follow. Practice solving these combinations mentally to increase your speed and accuracy in subtraction.

$\begin{array}{r}3\\-3\\\hline 0\end{array}$	$\begin{array}{r}5\\-5\\\hline 0\end{array}$	$\begin{array}{r}9\\-1\\\hline 8\end{array}$	$\begin{array}{r}6\\-3\\\hline 3\end{array}$	$\begin{array}{r}9\\-7\\\hline 2\end{array}$	$\begin{array}{r}9\\-9\\\hline 0\end{array}$	$\begin{array}{r}6\\-2\\\hline 4\end{array}$	$\begin{array}{r}9\\-4\\\hline 5\end{array}$	$\begin{array}{r}8\\-4\\\hline 4\end{array}$
$\begin{array}{r}5\\-2\\\hline 3\end{array}$	$\begin{array}{r}5\\-1\\\hline 4\end{array}$	$\begin{array}{r}4\\-4\\\hline 0\end{array}$	$\begin{array}{r}3\\-1\\\hline 2\end{array}$	$\begin{array}{r}3\\-2\\\hline 1\end{array}$	$\begin{array}{r}7\\-5\\\hline 2\end{array}$	$\begin{array}{r}6\\-5\\\hline 1\end{array}$	$\begin{array}{r}7\\-1\\\hline 6\end{array}$	$\begin{array}{r}9\\-6\\\hline 3\end{array}$
$\begin{array}{r}6\\-4\\\hline 2\end{array}$	$\begin{array}{r}4\\-3\\\hline 1\end{array}$	$\begin{array}{r}9\\-3\\\hline 6\end{array}$	$\begin{array}{r}8\\-1\\\hline 7\end{array}$	$\begin{array}{r}2\\-1\\\hline 1\end{array}$	$\begin{array}{r}8\\-6\\\hline 2\end{array}$	$\begin{array}{r}6\\-1\\\hline 5\end{array}$	$\begin{array}{r}8\\-3\\\hline 5\end{array}$	$\begin{array}{r}2\\-2\\\hline 0\end{array}$
$\begin{array}{r}7\\-4\\\hline 3\end{array}$	$\begin{array}{r}8\\-8\\\hline 0\end{array}$	$\begin{array}{r}8\\-2\\\hline 6\end{array}$	$\begin{array}{r}5\\-3\\\hline 2\end{array}$	$\begin{array}{r}7\\-2\\\hline 5\end{array}$	$\begin{array}{r}9\\-2\\\hline 7\end{array}$	$\begin{array}{r}7\\-7\\\hline 0\end{array}$	$\begin{array}{r}5\\-4\\\hline 1\end{array}$	$\begin{array}{r}1\\-1\\\hline 0\end{array}$
$\begin{array}{r}9\\-5\\\hline 4\end{array}$	$\begin{array}{r}4\\-1\\\hline 3\end{array}$	$\begin{array}{r}9\\-8\\\hline 1\end{array}$	$\begin{array}{r}7\\-3\\\hline 4\end{array}$	$\begin{array}{r}8\\-5\\\hline 3\end{array}$	$\begin{array}{r}7\\-6\\\hline 1\end{array}$	$\begin{array}{r}8\\-7\\\hline 1\end{array}$	$\begin{array}{r}4\\-2\\\hline 2\end{array}$	$\begin{array}{r}6\\-6\\\hline 0\end{array}$

8 Learning Activity

Subtract the following.

$\begin{array}{r}7\\-1\end{array}$	$\begin{array}{r}5\\-1\end{array}$	$\begin{array}{r}6\\-5\end{array}$	$\begin{array}{r}7\\-5\end{array}$	$\begin{array}{r}3\\-2\end{array}$
$\begin{array}{r}3\\-1\end{array}$	$\begin{array}{r}4\\-4\end{array}$	$\begin{array}{r}9\\-6\end{array}$	$\begin{array}{r}5\\-2\end{array}$	$\begin{array}{r}2\\-2\end{array}$
$\begin{array}{r}6\\-2\end{array}$	$\begin{array}{r}8\\-4\end{array}$	$\begin{array}{r}8\\-8\end{array}$	$\begin{array}{r}2\\-1\end{array}$	$\begin{array}{r}8\\-1\end{array}$
$\begin{array}{r}9\\-5\end{array}$	$\begin{array}{r}4\\-3\end{array}$	$\begin{array}{r}6\\-4\end{array}$	$\begin{array}{r}6\\-1\end{array}$	$\begin{array}{r}9\\-4\end{array}$
$\begin{array}{r}9\\-3\end{array}$	$\begin{array}{r}9\\-9\end{array}$	$\begin{array}{r}9\\-7\end{array}$	$\begin{array}{r}6\\-3\end{array}$	$\begin{array}{r}5\\-5\end{array}$
$\begin{array}{r}8\\-5\end{array}$	$\begin{array}{r}3\\-3\end{array}$	$\begin{array}{r}1\\-1\end{array}$	$\begin{array}{r}5\\-4\end{array}$	$\begin{array}{r}7\\-7\end{array}$

continued

$$\begin{array}{r} 7 \\ -\ 4 \\ \hline \end{array} \qquad \begin{array}{r} 7 \\ -\ 2 \\ \hline \end{array} \qquad \begin{array}{r} 9 \\ -\ 8 \\ \hline \end{array} \qquad \begin{array}{r} 8 \\ -\ 2 \\ \hline \end{array} \qquad \begin{array}{r} 8 \\ -\ 6 \\ \hline \end{array}$$

$$\begin{array}{r} 9 \\ -\ 2 \\ \hline \end{array} \qquad \begin{array}{r} 6 \\ -\ 6 \\ \hline \end{array} \qquad \begin{array}{r} 4 \\ -\ 2 \\ \hline \end{array} \qquad \begin{array}{r} 8 \\ -\ 7 \\ \hline \end{array} \qquad \begin{array}{r} 7 \\ -\ 6 \\ \hline \end{array}$$

$$\begin{array}{r} 9 \\ -\ 1 \\ \hline \end{array} \qquad \begin{array}{r} 7 \\ -\ 3 \\ \hline \end{array} \qquad \begin{array}{r} 5 \\ -\ 3 \\ \hline \end{array} \qquad \begin{array}{r} 4 \\ -\ 1 \\ \hline \end{array} \qquad \begin{array}{r} 8 \\ -\ 3 \\ \hline \end{array}$$

Subtracting One-Digit Numbers from Two-Digit Numbers

In the following subtraction problems, a one-digit number is subtracted from a two-digit number. Practice solving these combinations mentally to increase your speed and accuracy in subtraction.

$$\begin{array}{r} 17 \\ -\ 8 \\ \hline 9 \end{array} \quad \begin{array}{r} 12 \\ -\ 9 \\ \hline 3 \end{array} \quad \begin{array}{r} 13 \\ -\ 8 \\ \hline 5 \end{array} \quad \begin{array}{r} 12 \\ -\ 8 \\ \hline 4 \end{array} \quad \begin{array}{r} 16 \\ -\ 8 \\ \hline 8 \end{array} \quad \begin{array}{r} 11 \\ -\ 9 \\ \hline 2 \end{array} \quad \begin{array}{r} 15 \\ -\ 9 \\ \hline 6 \end{array}$$

$$\begin{array}{r} 11 \\ -\ 8 \\ \hline 3 \end{array} \quad \begin{array}{r} 13 \\ -\ 9 \\ \hline 4 \end{array} \quad \begin{array}{r} 12 \\ -\ 3 \\ \hline 9 \end{array} \quad \begin{array}{r} 16 \\ -\ 7 \\ \hline 9 \end{array} \quad \begin{array}{r} 13 \\ -\ 6 \\ \hline 7 \end{array} \quad \begin{array}{r} 11 \\ -\ 5 \\ \hline 6 \end{array} \quad \begin{array}{r} 11 \\ -\ 4 \\ \hline 7 \end{array}$$

$$\begin{array}{r} 14 \\ -\ 9 \\ \hline 5 \end{array} \quad \begin{array}{r} 14 \\ -\ 8 \\ \hline 6 \end{array} \quad \begin{array}{r} 12 \\ -\ 4 \\ \hline 8 \end{array} \quad \begin{array}{r} 12 \\ -\ 5 \\ \hline 7 \end{array} \quad \begin{array}{r} 14 \\ -\ 6 \\ \hline 8 \end{array} \quad \begin{array}{r} 11 \\ -\ 2 \\ \hline 9 \end{array} \quad \begin{array}{r} 17 \\ -\ 9 \\ \hline 8 \end{array}$$

$$\begin{array}{r} 15 \\ -\ 6 \\ \hline 9 \end{array} \quad \begin{array}{r} 13 \\ -\ 5 \\ \hline 8 \end{array} \quad \begin{array}{r} 13 \\ -\ 4 \\ \hline 9 \end{array} \quad \begin{array}{r} 11 \\ -\ 3 \\ \hline 8 \end{array} \quad \begin{array}{r} 15 \\ -\ 7 \\ \hline 8 \end{array} \quad \begin{array}{r} 11 \\ -\ 6 \\ \hline 5 \end{array} \quad \begin{array}{r} 14 \\ -\ 5 \\ \hline 9 \end{array}$$

$$\begin{array}{r} 15 \\ -\ 8 \\ \hline 7 \end{array} \quad \begin{array}{r} 14 \\ -\ 7 \\ \hline 7 \end{array} \quad \begin{array}{r} 18 \\ -\ 9 \\ \hline 9 \end{array} \quad \begin{array}{r} 16 \\ -\ 9 \\ \hline 7 \end{array} \quad \begin{array}{r} 13 \\ -\ 7 \\ \hline 6 \end{array} \quad \begin{array}{r} 12 \\ -\ 7 \\ \hline 5 \end{array} \quad \begin{array}{r} 11 \\ -\ 7 \\ \hline 4 \end{array}$$

9 Learning Activity

Subtract the following.

$$\begin{array}{r} 13 \\ -\ 6 \\ \hline \end{array} \quad \begin{array}{r} 11 \\ -\ 5 \\ \hline \end{array} \quad \begin{array}{r} 14 \\ -\ 6 \\ \hline \end{array} \quad \begin{array}{r} 16 \\ -\ 7 \\ \hline \end{array} \quad \begin{array}{r} 15 \\ -\ 7 \\ \hline \end{array} \quad \begin{array}{r} 15 \\ -\ 9 \\ \hline \end{array} \quad \begin{array}{r} 14 \\ -\ 9 \\ \hline \end{array}$$

$$\begin{array}{r} 12 \\ -\ 9 \\ \hline \end{array} \quad \begin{array}{r} 16 \\ -\ 8 \\ \hline \end{array} \quad \begin{array}{r} 11 \\ -\ 4 \\ \hline \end{array} \quad \begin{array}{r} 12 \\ -\ 5 \\ \hline \end{array} \quad \begin{array}{r} 12 \\ -\ 4 \\ \hline \end{array} \quad \begin{array}{r} 17 \\ -\ 9 \\ \hline \end{array} \quad \begin{array}{r} 11 \\ -\ 8 \\ \hline \end{array}$$

continued

$$\begin{array}{r}13\\-\ 7\\\hline\end{array}\qquad\begin{array}{r}11\\-\ 6\\\hline\end{array}\qquad\begin{array}{r}13\\-\ 9\\\hline\end{array}\qquad\begin{array}{r}11\\-\ 3\\\hline\end{array}\qquad\begin{array}{r}11\\-\ 9\\\hline\end{array}\qquad\begin{array}{r}13\\-\ 5\\\hline\end{array}\qquad\begin{array}{r}15\\-\ 6\\\hline\end{array}$$

$$\begin{array}{r}12\\-\ 3\\\hline\end{array}\qquad\begin{array}{r}13\\-\ 4\\\hline\end{array}\qquad\begin{array}{r}11\\-\ 2\\\hline\end{array}\qquad\begin{array}{r}12\\-\ 8\\\hline\end{array}\qquad\begin{array}{r}13\\-\ 8\\\hline\end{array}\qquad\begin{array}{r}14\\-\ 8\\\hline\end{array}\qquad\begin{array}{r}14\\-\ 7\\\hline\end{array}$$

$$\begin{array}{r}11\\-\ 7\\\hline\end{array}\qquad\begin{array}{r}12\\-\ 7\\\hline\end{array}\qquad\begin{array}{r}14\\-\ 5\\\hline\end{array}\qquad\begin{array}{r}17\\-\ 8\\\hline\end{array}\qquad\begin{array}{r}18\\-\ 9\\\hline\end{array}\qquad\begin{array}{r}16\\-\ 9\\\hline\end{array}\qquad\begin{array}{r}15\\-\ 8\\\hline\end{array}$$

Borrowing Numbers in Subtraction

Subtracting numbers that have more than one digit requires an understanding of borrowing numbers. For example, to subtract 67 from 94, first a 10 must be borrowed from the 90 making it 80. Then the 10 is added to the 4 making it 14. Now you can subtract 7 from 14 and 6 from 8, as shown below:

$$\begin{array}{r}{\scriptstyle 8\ 1}\\\cancel{9}\,4\\-\ 6\ 7\\\hline 2\ 7\end{array}\qquad\text{or}\qquad\begin{array}{r}8\\-\ 6\\\hline 2\end{array}\quad\begin{array}{r}14\\-\ 7\\\hline 7\end{array}$$

To subtract numbers that have more than two digits, follow the same procedure for each column. For example, to subtract 189 from 200, proceed as follows:

$$\begin{array}{r}{\scriptstyle 1\ 9\ 1}\\\cancel{2}\,\cancel{0}\,0\\-\ 1\ 8\ 9\\\hline 1\ 1\end{array}\qquad\text{or}\qquad\begin{array}{r}1\\-\ 1\\\hline 0\end{array}\quad\begin{array}{r}9\\-\ 8\\\hline 1\end{array}\quad\begin{array}{r}10\\-\ 9\\\hline 1\end{array}$$

Here are some other examples of borrowing numbers in subtraction:

$$\begin{array}{r}{\scriptstyle 8\ 1}\\\cancel{9}\,7\\-\ 1\ 8\\\hline 7\ 9\end{array}\qquad\begin{array}{r}{\scriptstyle 2\ 1}\\1\,\cancel{3}\,5\\-\ 6\ 7\\\hline 6\ 8\end{array}\qquad\begin{array}{r}{\scriptstyle 7\ 1}\\6\,\cancel{8}\,5\\-\ 4\ 6\ 6\\\hline 2\ 1\ 9\end{array}$$

$$\begin{array}{r}{\scriptstyle 7\ 13\ 1}\\\cancel{8}\,\cancel{4}\,1\\-\ 5\ 4\ 2\\\hline 2\ 9\ 9\end{array}\qquad\begin{array}{r}{\scriptstyle 3\ 9\ 1}\\\cancel{4}{,}\cancel{0}\,0\,9\\-\ 3{,}7\ 7\ 6\\\hline 2\ 3\ 3\end{array}\qquad\begin{array}{r}{\scriptstyle 8\ 1\ 7\ 1}\\\cancel{9}{,}\cancel{6}\,\cancel{8}\,4\\-\ 8{,}7\ 6\ 5\\\hline 9\ 1\ 9\end{array}$$

Subtract the following. Use borrowing when necessary.

73	81	81	52	83
− 46	− 66	− 19	− 36	− 37

197	365	883	902	113
− 139	− 208	− 329	− 624	− 88

4,748	5,052	3,006	1,763	35,290
− 3,759	− 3,086	− 1,008	− 884	− 8,765

Proving Your Answer in Subtraction

To prove your answer in subtraction, simply add the *subtrahend* (the number being subtracted) to the *difference* (the answer to the subtraction problem). The total should equal the *minuend* (the number being subtracted from). Look at the following example:

Minuend   8
Subtrahend − 5 ⎤ = 8   Total equals 8, which is the
Difference   3 ⎦   same as the minuend.

You can also check your answer by extending the subtraction to form an addition problem. For example:

+ ⎡   8,632 ⎤
   ⎣ − 4,466
       4,166 ⎦   Notice that these two numbers are the
       8,632   same, proving 4,166 is the correct answer.

Subtract the following and prove your answers.

8,376	989	632	2,161	3,577
− 3,567	− 765	− 176	− 783	− 1,864

417	494	766	9,842	3,870
− 338	− 77	− 489	− 1,856	− 1,399

Subtracting Decimals

The placement of the decimal point in subtraction is the same as in addition. The decimal points are always placed directly under one another. For example:

$$\begin{array}{r} \$1,767.59 \\ -\ 567.50 \\ \hline \$1,200.09 \end{array}$$

Decimal points are placed one under another when subtracting.

12
Learning Activity

Subtract the following. Correctly place the decimal point in the answer. Rewrite the problem if necessary.

$$\begin{array}{r} \$87.25 \\ -\ 7.65 \\ \hline \end{array} \qquad \begin{array}{r} \$133.95 \\ -\ 26.79 \\ \hline \end{array} \qquad \begin{array}{r} \$179.50 \\ -\ 25.76 \\ \hline \end{array}$$

$$\begin{array}{r} \$1.72 \\ -\ 0.75 \\ \hline \end{array} \qquad \begin{array}{r} \$17.98 \\ -\ 1.80 \\ \hline \end{array} \qquad \begin{array}{r} \$1,995.75 \\ -\ 86.87 \\ \hline \end{array}$$

$$\begin{array}{r} \$39.11 \\ -\ 29.22 \\ \hline \end{array} \qquad \begin{array}{r} \$79.50 \\ -\ 29.50 \\ \hline \end{array} \qquad \begin{array}{r} \$257.32 \\ -\ 8.59 \\ \hline \end{array}$$

MULTIPLYING CORRECTLY

Illus. 1-3

Stock people use multiplication to find the value of a business's inventory.

The Multiplication Tables

To multiply with speed and accuracy, you must memorize the multiplication combinations of 2 through 12. A second, but slower, way is to use a printed multiplication table. (Table 1-1 is a multiplication table of the numbers 2 through 25.) In the table, the answer to a multiplication problem is that number found at the point where the horizontal and vertical number columns cross. For example, to multiply 9 times 22, first find 9 in the horizontal column across the top of the table. Second, move down the table vertically to the number 22 column. The answer, 198, is given where the two columns cross. You will notice in the multiplication table that the numbers 2 through 12 have been shaded. These are the commonly used multiplication combinations you should memorize.

Table 1-1
Multiplication Table

	2	3	4	5	6	7	8	9	10	11	12	13	14	15	16	17	18	19	20	21	22	23	24	25
2	4	6	8	10	12	14	16	18	20	22	24	26	28	30	32	34	36	38	40	42	44	46	48	50
3	6	9	12	15	18	21	24	27	30	33	36	39	42	45	48	51	54	57	60	63	66	69	72	75
4	8	12	16	20	24	28	32	36	40	44	48	52	56	60	64	68	72	76	80	84	88	92	96	100
5	10	15	20	25	30	35	40	45	50	55	60	65	70	75	80	85	90	95	100	105	110	115	120	125
6	12	18	24	30	36	42	48	54	60	66	72	78	84	90	96	102	108	114	120	126	132	138	144	150
7	14	21	28	35	42	49	56	63	70	77	84	91	98	105	112	119	126	133	140	147	154	161	168	175
8	16	24	32	40	48	56	64	72	80	88	96	104	112	120	128	136	144	152	160	168	176	184	192	200
9	18	27	36	45	54	63	72	81	90	99	108	117	126	135	144	153	162	171	180	189	198	207	216	225
10	20	30	40	50	60	70	80	90	100	110	120	130	140	150	160	170	180	190	200	210	220	230	240	250
11	22	33	44	55	66	77	88	99	110	121	132	143	154	165	176	187	198	209	220	231	242	253	264	275
12	24	36	48	60	72	84	96	108	120	132	144	156	168	180	192	204	216	228	240	252	264	276	288	300
13	26	39	52	65	78	91	104	117	130	143	156	169	182	195	208	221	234	247	260	273	286	299	312	325
14	28	42	56	70	84	98	112	126	140	154	168	182	196	210	224	238	252	266	280	294	308	322	336	350
15	30	45	60	75	90	105	120	135	150	165	180	195	210	225	240	255	270	285	300	315	330	345	360	375
16	32	48	64	80	96	112	128	144	160	176	192	208	224	240	256	272	288	304	320	336	352	368	384	400
17	34	51	68	85	102	119	136	153	170	187	204	221	238	255	272	289	306	323	340	357	374	391	408	425
18	36	54	72	90	108	126	144	162	180	198	216	234	252	270	288	306	324	342	360	378	396	414	432	450
19	38	57	76	95	114	133	152	171	190	209	228	247	266	285	304	323	342	361	380	399	418	437	456	475
20	40	60	80	100	120	140	160	180	200	220	240	260	280	300	320	340	360	380	400	420	440	460	480	500
21	42	63	84	105	126	147	168	189	210	231	252	273	294	315	336	357	378	399	420	441	462	483	504	525
22	44	66	88	110	132	154	176	198	220	242	264	286	308	330	352	374	396	418	440	462	484	506	528	550
23	46	69	92	115	138	161	184	207	230	253	276	299	322	345	368	391	414	437	460	483	506	529	552	575
24	48	72	96	120	144	168	192	216	240	264	288	312	336	360	384	408	432	456	480	504	528	552	576	600
25	50	75	100	125	150	175	200	225	250	275	300	325	350	375	400	425	450	475	500	525	550	575	600	625

13
Learning Activity

Multiply the following using the multiplication table.

$10 \times 15 =$ $18 \times 16 =$ $6 \times 14 =$

$8 \times 6 =$ $19 \times 3 =$ $13 \times 13 =$

$24 \times 8 =$ $6 \times 7 =$ $3 \times 14 =$

$11 \times 19 =$ $7 \times 12 =$ $8 \times 23 =$

$25 \times 24 =$ $8 \times 19 =$ $25 \times 17 =$

Multiplying One-Digit and Two-Digit Numbers

When multiplying a two-digit number by a one-digit number, you must carry over a number. The number carried over should be written (lightly) by the next number to be multiplied. For example:

$$\begin{array}{r} {}^{1} \\ 83 \\ \times\ 6 \\ \hline 498 \end{array}$$

Step 1: $3 \times 6 = 18$, write down the 8 and carry the 1.

Step 2: $6 \times 8 = 48$; $48 + 1 = 49$

---

14 Learning Activity

Multiply the following correctly.

87	52	21	33	97	68	62
× 4	× 7	× 8	× 5	× 4	× 9	× 6

23	98	48	22	18	22	76
× 8	× 6	× 3	× 9	× 5	× 7	× 2

65	78	18	24	12	89	15
× 3	× 4	× 6	× 9	× 8	× 4	× 3

Multiplying Larger Numbers

When multiplying larger numbers, make sure that the numbers are placed correctly. The last number of each product must be directly below its multiplier in the problem. For example:

Correct

$$\begin{array}{r} {}^{2\ 4} \\ 97 \\ \times\ 46 \\ \hline 582 \\ 388 \\ \hline 4,462 \end{array}$$

← The multiplier is 6.
← The multiplier is 4.

Incorrect

$$\begin{array}{r} {}^{2\ 4} \\ 97 \\ \times\ 46 \\ \hline 582 \\ 388 \\ \hline 39,382 \end{array}$$

Multiply the following correctly.

73	88	33	15	95
× 42	× 18	× 51	× 18	× 88

27	56	67	77	59
× 14	× 18	× 16	× 36	× 43

65	98	29	74	28
× 18	× 12	× 13	× 32	× 15

53	18	21	38	16
× 17	× 26	× 17	× 38	× 79

Proving Your Answer in Multiplication

Two methods can be used to check the accuracy of multiplication. In the first method, divide the *product* (answer) by the *multiplicand* (top number) in your problem. The result of this division will equal the *multiplier* (second number). For example:

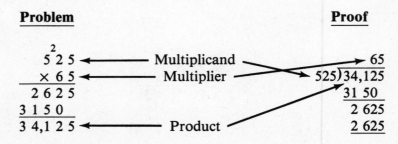

To use the second method, reverse the numbers in the multiplication problem and multiply a second time. For example:

	Problem		Proof
	525		65
	× 65		× 525
	2625		325
	3150		130
	34,125		325
			34,125

16
Learning Activity

Multiply the following and check the accuracy of your answers using either of the methods explained above.

432	525	849	67
× 63	× 15	× 18	× 42

117	223	345	680
× 93	× 7	× 49	× 27

56	178	214	385
× 38	× 53	× 17	× 98

33	52	1,042	2,965
× 33	× 43	× 168	× 532

1,890	1,050	2,765	1,327
× 79	× 98	× 138	× 327

Multiplying Decimals

To multiply a decimal by a whole number or a decimal by a decimal, add the number of digits to the right of each decimal point in the problem. Then in the answer, count from right to left that total number of decimal places and place the decimal point.

Decimal × Whole Number

Multiply: $7.95 × 6

Solution: $7.95 ◄── 2 Digits
              × 6
              ─────
              $47.70
                 ▲
                 └─── 2 Decimal Places

Decimal × Decimal

Multiply: $62.75 × 0.5

Solution: $62.75 ◄── 2 Digits
              × 0.5 ◄── 1 Digit
              ───────
              $31.375
                  ▲
                  └─── 3 Decimal Places

17
Learning Activity

Multiply the following. Place the decimal point in the correct location in your answer.

| $12.50 | $63.00 | 55.95 | 6.75 |
| × 7 | × 0.40 | × 10 | × 0.33 |

| 3,141.50 | $7.95 | $67.50 | $199.00 |
| × 12 | × 0.40 | × 0.8 | × 0.50 |

| $13.95 | $39.50 | $88.00 | $799.99 |
| × 0.20 | × 16 | × 0.17 | × 0.67 |

continued

$168.50	$69.78	2,995.50	187.59
× 0.08	× 18	× 0.50	× 0.15

15.95	21.78	$14.75	$18.75
× 27	× 8	× 0.33	× 0.27

DIVIDING CORRECTLY

Illus. 1-4

Sales clerks may need to use division to find unit prices.

Basic Division Review

How many times is one number contained in another? Division is the operation used to find out. Division is the opposite of multiplication. For example:

$$5 \times 7 = 35 \qquad 35 \div 7 = 5$$

In division, the number being divided (35) is called the *dividend*. The number doing the dividing (7) is called the *divisor*. The answer (5) is referred to as the *quotient*.

$$\text{Divisor} \rightarrow 7\overline{)35} \quad \begin{array}{l} \nwarrow \text{Quotient (Answer)} \\ \nwarrow \text{Dividend} \end{array}$$

Short Division

When dividing by a one-digit number, short division is usually used. In short division write only the quotient at the top of the division problem. For example:

$$3\overline{)363} = 121$$

Sometimes in short division, it is necessary to carry numbers that represent the amount left over after the first partial division. These numbers are written lightly to the left of the next digit in the division problem. For example:

$$5\overline{)8{}^36{}^17{}^20} = 1{,}7\,3\,4$$

18
Learning Activity

Divide the following using short division.

$8\overline{)592}$	$6\overline{)360}$	$7\overline{)497}$	$5\overline{)250}$
$8\overline{)648}$	$3\overline{)309}$	$6\overline{)420}$	$2\overline{)222}$
$7\overline{)553}$	$8\overline{)640}$	$9\overline{)459}$	$6\overline{)4{,}230}$
$7\overline{)3{,}549}$	$3\overline{)1{,}800}$	$6\overline{)3{,}420}$	$5\overline{)3{,}555}$
$5\overline{)3{,}020}$	$2\overline{)2{,}104}$	$7\overline{)6{,}377}$	$9\overline{)18{,}018}$

Long Division

When dividing by a number with two or more digits, it is usually necessary to use long division. This means that each step is written down as shown below:

$$
\begin{array}{r}
1{,}141\tfrac{8}{67} \\
67\overline{)76{,}455} \\
\underline{67} \\
9\,4 \\
\underline{6\,7} \\
2\,75 \\
\underline{2\,68} \\
75 \\
\underline{67} \\
8 \leftarrow \text{Remainder (Left Over)}
\end{array}
$$

Note that the number 8 is left over in the example. This number is called the remainder and is expressed as a fractional part of the divisor 67, or $\frac{8}{67}$.

In some division problems the remainder may be a fraction that can be reduced. For example, if the remainder of a division problem is 8 and the divisor is 64, the remainder will be $\frac{8}{64}$. This can be reduced by dividing the numerator and denominator by 8, resulting in a reduced fraction of $\frac{1}{8}$. Remember to always reduce the fraction by dividing the numerator and denominator by the largest possible whole number. Divide both the numerator and denominator by the same number. This procedure will reduce the fraction to *lowest terms*. Practice reducing the following fractions before completing Learning Activity 20.

19
Learning Activity

Reduce to lowest terms.

$\frac{4}{16} =$ $\frac{21}{63} =$ $\frac{3}{15} =$

$\frac{8}{12} =$ $\frac{200}{220} =$ $\frac{5}{30} =$

$\frac{10}{80} =$ $\frac{6}{33} =$ $\frac{25}{50} =$

20
Learning Activity

Find the quotient for each problem using long division. Reduce any remainders to lowest terms.

$25\overline{)376}$ $37\overline{)5,857}$ $55\overline{)895}$

$16\overline{)3,645}$ $98\overline{)39,800}$ $33\overline{)7,695}$

continued

$$90\overline{)1{,}090} \qquad 54\overline{)13{,}678} \qquad 63\overline{)2{,}037}$$

$$35\overline{)672} \qquad 7\overline{)846} \qquad 74\overline{)2{,}665}$$

$$60\overline{)3{,}390} \qquad 12\overline{)36{,}500} \qquad 18\overline{)8{,}664}$$

Proving Your Answer in Division

To prove your answer in division, just multiply the quotient by the divisor and add the remainder.

Problem	Proof

```
                1,141  ← Quotient
Divisor → 67)76,455
              67
               9 4
               6 7
               2 75
               2 68
                 75
                 67
                  8  ← Remainder
```

```
1,141  ← Quotient
× 67   ← Divisor
7 987
68 46
76,447
+ 8    ← Remainder
76,455
```

Divide the following and prove your answers.

$7\overline{)595}$ $\qquad$ $80\overline{)760}$ $\qquad$ $54\overline{)654}$

$12\overline{)1,867}$ $\qquad$ $16\overline{)756}$ $\qquad$ $6\overline{)549}$

$8\overline{)648}$ $\qquad$ $91\overline{)987}$ $\qquad$ $220\overline{)9,440}$

$17\overline{)1,618}$ $\qquad$ $63\overline{)828}$ $\qquad$ $33\overline{)7,197}$

$81\overline{)6,894}$ $\qquad$ $450\overline{)28,750}$ $\qquad$ $35\overline{)4,137}$

Dividing Decimals

When the dividend contains a decimal point and the divisor is a whole number, place the decimal point in the answer directly above the decimal point in the dividend. Place the decimal point in the quotient (answer) before you actually complete the long division. For example:

```
                        Decimal Point
                            |
                          $2.10  ← Quotient (Answer)
        Divisor → 6)$12.60       ← Dividend
                    12
                     6
                     6
                     0
                     0
```

When the divisor has a decimal point, you cannot proceed until the decimal point is relocated so that the divisor becomes a whole number. You must move the decimal point in the dividend the same number of places as you did in the divisor, adding zeros if necessary. Finally, place the decimal point in the quotient (answer) directly over the new location of the decimal point in the dividend. For example:

```
                           2 92.      ← Quotient (Answer)
        Divisor → 1.25.)366.00.      ← Dividend
                       250
                       116 0
                       112 5
                         3 50
                         2 50
                         1 00
```

Note that there was a remainder of 100 in this division problem. To show this as a decimal fraction in the answer, add zeros to the dividend (after the decimal point) and continue to divide. For example:

```
                       2 92.8
        1.25.)366.00.0
              250
              116 0
              112 5
                3 50
                2 50
                1 00 0
                1 00 0
```

Rounding in Division

In some division problems, it may be necessary to round the answers. In division problems that do not involve money, the common rule is to round to the next highest number when the number in the thousandths place is 5 or larger. Drop the number in the thousandths place when it is 4 or less. For example, to divide 11.8 by 6, proceed as shown:

$$
\begin{array}{r}
1.966 \\
6)\overline{11.800} \\
\underline{6} \\
5\,8 \\
\underline{5\,4} \\
40 \\
\underline{36} \\
40 \\
\underline{36}
\end{array}
$$

The correct answer rounded to the nearest hundredth is 1.97.

22 Learning Activity

Divide the following. Place the decimal point in the correct location in each answer. Round your answers to the nearest hundredth.

$$0.40)\overline{220.00} \qquad 2.2)\overline{7.63} \qquad 0.25)\overline{1{,}255.00}$$

$$2.75)\overline{37.60} \qquad 89)\overline{917.70} \qquad 67)\overline{356.50}$$

$$0.25)\overline{197.00} \qquad 2.03)\overline{11{,}874.60} \qquad 0.97)\overline{98.27}$$

continued

$$0.40\overline{)765.40} \qquad 52\overline{)840.00} \qquad 33.3\overline{)79.95}$$

$$3\overline{)216.60} \qquad 7.6\overline{)187.0} \qquad 1.10\overline{)97.67}$$

Rounding Dollars and Cents

In division problems that involve dollars and cents, the accepted rule in division is that all rounding is done to the benefit of the business. For example, items sold by a business at 3 for $1.00 would be sold for 34¢ each instead of 33¢. Businesses always round up to the next whole cent. Remember to always round in the business's favor when dividing in business.

23
Learning Activity

Solve the following problems. Round in the business's favor.

1. A case of canned tuna sells for $33.95 per case. There are 24 cans in each case. What would the business charge for each can of tuna?

_____

2. A supermarket sells bananas at $2.67 for five pounds. How much would they charge customers for one pound?

_____

Averages

To find an average for a set of numbers or items, first find the sum. Then divide this total by the number of items. For example, if you were asked to find the average sales for a six-month period, you would total the sales for that six-month period and then divide that total by six.

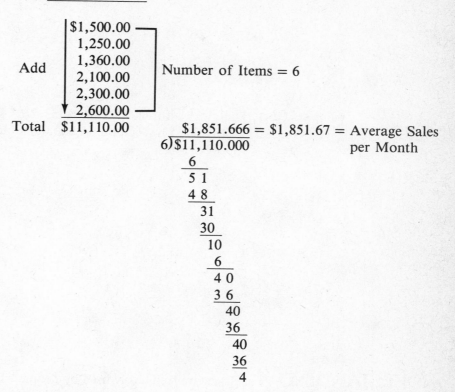

Six-Month Sales

Add
$1,500.00
1,250.00
1,360.00
2,100.00
2,300.00
2,600.00

Number of Items = 6

Total $11,110.00

$$\begin{array}{r} \$1,851.666 = \$1,851.67 = \text{Average Sales} \\ 6)\overline{\$11,110.000} \qquad \qquad \text{per Month} \\ \underline{6} \\ 5\,1 \\ \underline{4\,8} \\ 31 \\ \underline{30} \\ 10 \\ \underline{6} \\ 4\,0 \\ \underline{3\,6} \\ 40 \\ \underline{36} \\ 40 \\ \underline{36} \\ 4 \end{array}$$

24
Learning Activity

1. Gebhart's Department Store has four departments. During the year, sales for the Sporting Goods Department were $15,876; Shoe Department, $9,675; Apparel Department, $28,700; and Housewares Department, $18,450. Find the average sales for those four departments.

_____

continued

2. The number of customers on each day of one week was 376, 971, 1,042, 674, 850, 654, and 525. Find the average number of customers per day.

_____

3. Daily sales for a week were $3,576, $987.72, $550.00, $1,560.75, $2,187.00, $3,176, and $4,050.00. Find the average daily sales for the week.

_____

UNDERSTANDING FRACTIONS AND PERCENTAGE FRACTIONS

Illus. 1-5

An understanding of fractions is often necessary for finding prices of sale items.

Fractions are frequently used by people who work in marketing occupations. When a single unit or number is divided into equal parts, each part is expressed as a fraction of the whole. The circles in Figure 1-1 illustrate fractional parts.

Figure 1-1
Fractional Parts

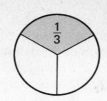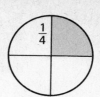

Adding Fractions with the Same Denominator

Fractions with the same *denominator* (bottom number) are easy to add. Simply add the *numerators* (top numbers) and place this sum over the denominator. Then, when possible, reduce the answer (resulting fraction) to the smallest number you can by dividing the numerator and denominator by the same number.

$$\frac{1}{2} + \frac{1}{2} = \frac{2}{2} = 1$$

$$\frac{1}{4} + \frac{1}{4} = \frac{2}{4} = \frac{1}{2}$$

$$\frac{1}{3} + \frac{1}{3} = \frac{2}{3}$$

$$\frac{1}{8} + \frac{1}{8} = \frac{2}{8} = \frac{1}{4}$$

$$\frac{1}{5} + \frac{3}{5} = \frac{4}{5}$$

$$\frac{3}{16} + \frac{5}{16} = \frac{8}{16} = \frac{1}{2}$$

25
Learning Activity

Add the following fractions.

$$\frac{1}{3} + \frac{2}{3}$$

$$\frac{1}{8} + \frac{3}{8}$$

$$\frac{1}{4} + \frac{1}{4}$$

$$\frac{5}{8} + \frac{1}{8}$$

$$\frac{6}{16} + \frac{5}{16}$$

$$\frac{1}{2} + \frac{1}{2}$$

$$\frac{3}{16} + \frac{7}{16}$$

$$\frac{1}{8} + \frac{1}{8}$$

$$\frac{3}{4} + \frac{1}{4}$$

$$\frac{1}{3} + \frac{1}{3}$$

$$\frac{1}{16} + \frac{14}{16}$$

$$\frac{3}{8} + \frac{4}{8}$$

$$\frac{1}{5} + \frac{2}{5}$$

$$\frac{2}{5} + \frac{2}{5}$$

$$\frac{1}{8} + \frac{6}{8}$$

Adding Fractions with Different Denominators

To add fractions that have different denominators, you must find a common denominator first. A common denominator is a number into which each of the denominators will divide without a remainder. To further simplify the addition of fractions, find the lowest common denominator. This is the smallest number divisible by each denominator in the problem. Once the lowest common denominator has been determined, the denominator of each fraction is then divided into this common denominator. The result is multiplied by the numerator. Look at the two examples below.

Example 1

$$\frac{1}{6} = \frac{1}{6} \leftarrow \text{Lowest Common}$$
$$\frac{1}{2} = \frac{3}{6} \qquad \text{Denominator}$$
$$+\frac{1}{3} = \frac{2}{6}$$
$$\frac{6}{6} = 1$$

Example 2

$$\frac{1}{4} = \frac{5}{20} \leftarrow \text{Lowest Common}$$
$$\frac{1}{2} = \frac{10}{20} \qquad \text{Denominator}$$
$$+\frac{1}{5} = \frac{4}{20}$$
$$\frac{19}{20}$$

26 Learning Activity

Add the following fractions by finding the lowest common denominators.

$$\frac{1}{2} \qquad \frac{1}{8} \qquad \frac{2}{3} \qquad \frac{3}{16} \qquad \frac{2}{5}$$
$$+\frac{1}{3} \qquad +\frac{1}{16} \qquad +\frac{1}{4} \qquad +\frac{1}{2} \qquad +\frac{3}{20}$$

$$\frac{1}{12} \qquad \frac{1}{3} \qquad \frac{1}{8} \qquad \frac{1}{6} \qquad \frac{1}{10}$$
$$\frac{1}{3} \qquad \frac{1}{9} \qquad \frac{1}{12} \qquad \frac{1}{3} \qquad \frac{1}{5}$$
$$+\frac{1}{4} \qquad +\frac{1}{9} \qquad +\frac{1}{4} \qquad +\frac{1}{2} \qquad +\frac{1}{20}$$

$$\frac{3}{8} \qquad \frac{2}{3} \qquad \frac{1}{5} \qquad \frac{5}{12} \qquad \frac{1}{5}$$
$$+\frac{5}{16} \qquad +\frac{1}{12} \qquad +\frac{1}{10} \qquad +\frac{1}{4} \qquad +\frac{1}{2}$$

Improper Fractions and Mixed Numbers

Many times when fractions are added, the answer may have a numerator greater than its denominator. This fraction is called an *improper fraction*. ($\frac{12}{8}$ is an example of an improper fraction.) This must be changed to a whole number and a fraction. To do this, divide the numerator by the denominator. The improper fraction $\frac{12}{8}$ can be changed to the whole number 1 plus the fraction $\frac{4}{8}$ or $\frac{1}{2}$. The answer, $1\frac{1}{2}$, is called a *mixed number*.

27
Learning Activity

Convert the following improper fractions to mixed numbers.

$\frac{12}{4} =$ $\frac{6}{4} =$ $\frac{4}{3} =$ $\frac{12}{8} =$ $\frac{6}{5} =$

$\frac{9}{6} =$ $\frac{8}{3} =$ $\frac{9}{5} =$ $\frac{10}{6} =$ $\frac{24}{7} =$

$\frac{8}{6} =$ $\frac{9}{7} =$ $\frac{14}{8} =$ $\frac{8}{7} =$ $\frac{3}{2} =$

$\frac{17}{6} =$ $\frac{5}{4} =$ $\frac{9}{4} =$ $\frac{15}{6} =$ $\frac{13}{5} =$

Adding Mixed Numbers

Remember that a mixed number consists of a whole number and a fraction. To add mixed numbers, first add the fractions and then the whole numbers. Be sure all fractions have a common denominator. Change them if they do not.

$$3\frac{1}{3} = 3\frac{2}{6}$$
$$7\frac{1}{2} = 7\frac{3}{6}$$
$$\underline{+\ 9\frac{5}{6}} = \underline{9\frac{5}{6}}$$
$$19\frac{10}{6} \longrightarrow \frac{10}{6} = 1\frac{4}{6} = 1\frac{2}{3}$$
$$19 + 1\frac{2}{3} = 20\frac{2}{3}$$

Add the following mixed numbers.

$17\frac{1}{2}$ $186\frac{1}{4}$ $5\frac{3}{16}$ $35\frac{1}{3}$

$23\frac{3}{4}$ $+\ 78\frac{5}{8}$ $17\frac{1}{4}$ $+\ 26\frac{1}{8}$

$+\ 14\frac{1}{8}$ $+\ 21\frac{5}{8}$

$134\frac{1}{3}$ $75\frac{1}{10}$ $196\frac{1}{2}$ $397\frac{5}{8}$

$+\ 145\frac{5}{6}$ $+\ 16\frac{3}{20}$ $+\ 75\frac{1}{12}$ $+\ 27\frac{3}{16}$

Subtracting Fractions

When subtracting fractions that have the same denominator, subtract the numerators to find the answer. For example, to find the difference between $\frac{2}{5}$ and $\frac{3}{5}$, subtract the $\frac{2}{5}$ from the $\frac{3}{5}$. This is shown below.

$$\begin{array}{r} \frac{3}{5} \\ -\ \frac{2}{5} \\ \hline \frac{1}{5} \end{array} \qquad \text{Subtract Numerators:} \\ 3 - 2 = 1$$

To subtract fractions that have different denominators, you must convert to a common denominator, the same as in addition. For example, to find the difference between $\frac{1}{3}$ and $\frac{5}{7}$:

$$\begin{array}{rcl} \frac{5}{7} & = & \frac{15}{21} \leftarrow \text{Lowest Common} \\ -\ \frac{1}{3} & = & -\ \frac{7}{21} \quad \text{Denominator} \\ & & \frac{8}{21} \end{array}$$

When subtracting mixed numbers, first change each mixed number to an improper fraction. Second, convert the improper fractions to equivalent fractions with common denominators. Then, subtract the simple fractions. Finally, reduce the fractional answer to its lowest terms or to a mixed number.

For example, to subtract $2\frac{1}{2}$ from $5\frac{1}{4}$:

1st	2nd	3rd

$$5\frac{1}{4} = \frac{21}{4}$$
$$-\,2\frac{1}{2} = -\frac{5}{2}$$

$$\frac{21}{4} = \frac{21}{4}$$
$$-\frac{5}{2} = -\frac{10}{4}$$

$$\frac{21}{4}$$
$$-\frac{10}{4}$$
$$\frac{11}{4} = 2\frac{3}{4}$$

29
Learning Activity

Subtract the following fractions and mixed numbers.

$$\frac{3}{4}$$
$$-\frac{1}{2}$$
$$\qquad$$
$$\frac{2}{3}$$
$$-\frac{1}{3}$$
$$\qquad$$
$$\frac{5}{16}$$
$$-\frac{1}{8}$$

$$3\frac{3}{4}$$
$$-\,1\frac{1}{2}$$
$$\qquad$$
$$18\frac{5}{8}$$
$$-\,16\frac{1}{4}$$
$$\qquad$$
$$17\frac{3}{16}$$
$$-\,15\frac{5}{8}$$

$$275\frac{3}{4}$$
$$-\,75\frac{1}{2}$$
$$\qquad$$
$$12\frac{1}{8}$$
$$-\,11\frac{7}{12}$$
$$\qquad$$
$$14\frac{2}{3}$$
$$-\,8\frac{7}{8}$$

$$11\frac{3}{5}$$
$$-\,7\frac{1}{2}$$
$$\qquad$$
$$32\frac{1}{8}$$
$$-\,25\frac{1}{12}$$
$$\qquad$$
$$13\frac{2}{3}$$
$$-\,3\frac{1}{2}$$

Multiplying Fractions

To multiply fractions, first multiply the numerators and then multiply the denominators. When this step is completed, reduce the fraction to its lowest terms. For example:

Example 1: $\frac{3}{4} \times \frac{1}{2} = \frac{3}{8}$ **Example 2:** $5 \times \frac{1}{2} = \frac{5}{1} \times \frac{1}{2} = \frac{5}{2} = 2\frac{1}{2}$

To multiply a mixed number times a fraction or one mixed number times another, change the mixed number to an improper fraction. Then multiply the numerators and denominators as shown above. Again, make sure to reduce the fraction to its lowest terms or to a mixed number. For example:

Example 1: $2\frac{1}{2} \times 3\frac{2}{3} = \frac{5}{2} \times \frac{11}{3} = \frac{55}{6} = 9\frac{1}{6}$

Example 2: $25\frac{1}{3} \times 2\frac{1}{4} = \frac{76}{3} \times \frac{9}{4} = \frac{684}{12} = 57$

30
Learning Activity

Multiply the following fractions and mixed numbers.

$\frac{7}{8} \times \frac{1}{2} =$ $\qquad$ $\frac{1}{4} \times \frac{3}{4} =$

$5\frac{1}{4} \times 10\frac{1}{2} =$ $\qquad$ $1\frac{1}{2} \times 3\frac{1}{2} =$

$6\frac{1}{3} \times 2\frac{1}{3} =$ $\qquad$ $18\frac{1}{2} \times \frac{1}{3} =$

$10\frac{1}{4} \times 3\frac{1}{8} =$ $\qquad$ $4\frac{1}{2} \times 6\frac{1}{8} =$

$16 \times \frac{1}{4} =$ $\qquad$ $5\frac{1}{2} \times \frac{1}{5} =$

$\$4.20 \times \frac{1}{7} =$ $\qquad$ $\$3.25 \times \frac{1}{5} =$

Dividing Fractions

When dividing a whole number by a fraction or a fraction by a whole number, first express the whole number as a fraction with a denominator of 1. Second, invert the divisor. Third, multiply the numerators and the denominators. This procedure works when the divisor is a simple fraction, a whole number, or a mixed number. For example:

Example 1: $55 \div \frac{3}{5} = \frac{55}{1} \times \frac{5}{3} = \frac{275}{3} = 91\frac{2}{3}$

Example 2: $\frac{1}{5} \div \frac{2}{5} = \frac{1}{5} \times \frac{5}{2} = \frac{5}{10} = \frac{1}{2}$

Example 3: $1\frac{1}{2} \div 2\frac{2}{3} = \frac{3}{2} \div \frac{8}{3} = \frac{3}{2} \times \frac{3}{8} = \frac{9}{16}$

Divide the following fractions and mixed numbers by inverting the divisor and multiplying.

$24 \div \dfrac{3}{4} =$ $\qquad$ $\dfrac{5}{9} \div \dfrac{2}{3} =$

$\dfrac{7}{8} \div \dfrac{1}{3} =$ $\qquad$ $\dfrac{1}{10} \div \dfrac{3}{2} =$

$14\dfrac{1}{4} \div 7\dfrac{1}{8} =$ $\qquad$ $2\dfrac{1}{4} \div 1\dfrac{3}{4} =$

$\dfrac{1}{2} \div 5 =$ $\qquad$ $\dfrac{3}{8} \div \dfrac{1}{3} =$

$5\dfrac{1}{2} \div 3\dfrac{1}{2} =$ $\qquad$ $5\dfrac{1}{2} \div 5 =$

$28\dfrac{3}{4} \div 6\dfrac{7}{8} =$ $\qquad$ $100\dfrac{1}{4} \div 5\dfrac{1}{4} =$

$\$16.50 \div \dfrac{1}{5} =$ $\qquad$ $\$112.40 \div 1\dfrac{3}{4} =$

Percentages

Illus. 1-6

Percentages are often used in advertising sales.

Percentages are easy to understand when compared with common fractions and decimal fractions. Decimal fractions are obtained from common fractions by dividing the numerator of the common fraction by its denominator. For example:

$$\frac{1}{4} = 4\overline{)\begin{array}{c} 0.25 \\ 1.00 \\ \underline{8} \\ 20 \\ \underline{20} \end{array}} \leftarrow \text{Decimal Fraction}$$

Given below are percentage conversions for the most commonly used percentages. You should become familiar with them.

To change a decimal fraction to a percentage, simply move the decimal point two places to the right and add a percent (%) sign. (Note: If there is no decimal remainder after the decimal point is moved, the decimal point is understood and does not need to be shown.)

Fraction	Decimal Fraction	Percentage
$\frac{1}{2}$	0.50	50%
$\frac{1}{4}$	0.25	25%
$\frac{3}{4}$	0.75	75%
$\frac{1}{3}$	$0.33\frac{1}{3}$	$33\frac{1}{3}\%$
$\frac{2}{3}$	$0.66\frac{2}{3}$	$66\frac{2}{3}\%$
$\frac{1}{5}$	0.20	20%
$\frac{2}{5}$	0.40	40%
$\frac{3}{5}$	0.60	60%
$\frac{4}{5}$	0.80	80%

32
Learning Activity

Convert the following fractions to decimal fractions and percentages.

Fraction	Decimal Fraction	Percentage
$\frac{1}{10}$	_____	_____
$\frac{1}{5}$	_____	_____
$\frac{1}{6}$	_____	_____

continued

Fraction	Decimal Fraction	Percentage
$\frac{1}{2}$	_____	_____
$\frac{1}{3}$	_____	_____
$\frac{4}{5}$	_____	_____
$\frac{1}{8}$	_____	_____
$\frac{2}{3}$	_____	_____
$\frac{3}{8}$	_____	_____
$\frac{3}{4}$	_____	_____
$\frac{2}{5}$	_____	_____

Multiplying a Percentage Times a Whole Number

Multiplying a percentage times a whole number requires that the percentage first be changed to a decimal fraction. For example, to multiply 50 percent times the whole number $150:

$$\begin{array}{r} \$150 \\ \times\ 0.50 \\ \hline \$75.00 \end{array}$$

When multiplying a whole number by a percentage such as $33\frac{1}{3}\%$ or $66\frac{2}{3}\%$, there are two approaches that can be used to arrive at the correct answer. For example, if you were to multiply $600 by $33\frac{1}{3}\%$, you would:

Method 1: **Step 1:** Change $33\frac{1}{3}\%$ to the common fraction $\frac{1}{3}$.

Step 2: Multiply $600 \times \frac{1}{3} = \$200$.

Method 2: If you are using a calculator, multiply $600 \times 0.33333 = \$199.998$; rounded, this equals $200. When using a calculator, count the number of digits in the whole number and add two digits. Use this sum as the number of digits in the decimal fraction that you enter into your calculator. For example, $600 has three digits; add two more digits and use the five-digit decimal fraction 0.33(333).

Multiply the following percentages times the whole numbers given. Rewrite the problems, converting the percentages to decimal fractions or common fractions.

275 × 20%	100 × 75%	1,280 × 50%

\$129.50 × 40%	\$33 × 33⅓%	\$525 × 40%

\$125 × 25%	1,180 × 75%	\$300 × 66⅔%

\$5.50 × 50%	\$79.50 × 10%	\$13.60 × 66⅔%

\$6,796.00 × 25%	\$10,895 × 33⅓%	\$9,832 × 40%

SECTION 1
USING MATH IN MARKETING

1. Complete the following addition problems and check the accuracy of your answers.

a.	b.	c.	d.
17	275	$195.95	$4,286.00
23	222	+ 79.95	+ 2,344.00
14	88		
16	+ 171		
+ 18			

e.	f.	g.	h.
$59.50	$21.30	$3,640.00	$105.85
+ 26.75	19.85	+ 1,360.00	102.70
	22.05		130.80
	+ 25.40		+ 113.70

i. The Aquarium Fish Shop had sales of $3,000 for January, $2,655 for February, $2,100.45 for March, $1,875.00 for April, $2,735.37 for May, and $3,700.09 for June. Find the total sales for the six-month period.

$ _____

j. Add the following sales correctly. Check the accuracy of your answers.

Sales Check

Quantity	Description	Amount	
1	Suit	$179	95
1	Shirt	18	50
1	Tie	10	00
1	Pair Pants	30	00
	Total		

Sales Check

Quantity	Description	Amount	
1	Tackle Box	$24	95
1	Fishing Rod and Reel	39	94
1	Outdoor PVC Boots	12	95
1	Lure	2	95
	Total		

2. Complete the following subtraction problems and check the accuracy of your answers.

a.   82
    − 63

b.   746
    − 499

c. $277.95
    − 27.79

d. $4,617.45
    − 1,816.56

e. $235.85
    − 36.95

f. $1,285.05
    − 204.10

g.   62.39
    − 5.99

h. $1,466.50
    − 803.76

i. Steinbeck Fashions had total sales of $27,900 and expenses of $19,000 for the year. Find the difference between sales and expenses.

$_____

j. While Tara Smith was on a buying trip for her department store, she spent the following amounts: hotel and lodging, $88.76; meals, $40.30; tips, $7.60; taxis, $5.65; and telephone calls, $4.55. If Ms. Smith started out with $200 in cash, how much did she have left after her trip?

$_____

3. Complete the following multiplication problems. Check the accuracy of your answers.

a. 275
  × 8

b.   675
  × 23

c. $27.50
  × 0.05

d. $550.95
  × 27

e. $3.09
  × 14

f. $2,865.45
  × 0.20

g. $328.95
  × 0.25

h. $2,865.50
  × 13

Name _____

i. Do the necessary multiplication for each of the following sales. Add the total prices.

Quantity	Merchandise		Price	Total Price
5	Socks	@	$4.79	$ _____
2	Ties	@	$12.95	$ _____
6	Shirts	@	$25.00	$ _____
1	Sports coat	@	$99.00	$ _____
3	Slacks	@	$32.00	$ _____
			Total	$ _____

j. Larry Blaise was paid $4.25 per hour for working at Cache Recreation Rentals. If he worked nine hours on Monday, six on Tuesday, seven on Wednesday, seven on Thursday, and eight on Friday, how much would his total pay be for the week?

$ _____

4. Complete the following division problems. Express the answers to **a** through **d** in fraction form and round the answers to **e** through **h** to the nearest hundredth. Check the accuracy of your answers.

a. $4\overline{)216}$ b. $8\overline{)648}$ c. $16\overline{)5,880}$ d. $57\overline{)516}$

e. $150\overline{)27,500}$ f. $\$27.50\overline{)68}$ g. $64\overline{)\$776.60}$ h. $97\overline{)\$104.89}$

i. Total yearly sales for Jake's Sports were $324,000. What was the average monthly sales?

$ _____

j. The Byerite Grocery Store made the following purchases of cases of can goods. Find the cost per can to the nearest whole cent for each case.

No. of Cans in Case	Total Cost	Cost per Can
24	$5.76	$_____
46	$9.96	$_____
18	$6.25	$_____
18	$9.57	$_____
36	$10.95	$_____
36	$16.75	$_____
48	$28.90	$_____
48	$32.40	$_____

5. Complete the following fraction and percentage problems. Check the accuracy of your answers.

a. $\frac{2}{5} + \frac{1}{5} =$

b. $5\frac{1}{4} + 4\frac{3}{4} =$

c. $\frac{3}{5} + \frac{5}{12} + \frac{1}{4} =$

d. $\frac{5}{2} - \frac{2}{7} =$

e. $\frac{3}{4} - \frac{2}{3} =$

f. $82 - 62\frac{1}{2} =$

g. $2.75 \times 2\frac{1}{2} =$

h. $\frac{7}{8} \div \frac{5}{6} =$

i. $16.50 \div \frac{1}{4} =$

j. $7\frac{3}{4} - 6\frac{1}{4} =$

k. $3\frac{1}{2} \times 6\frac{5}{8} =$

l. $62.75 \times 10\frac{5}{8} =$

m. $24\frac{1}{2} \div 1\frac{1}{8} =$

n. $4.50 \div \frac{2}{3} =$

Name _____

o. Convert the following fractions to decimal fractions and percentages.

Fraction	Decimal Fraction	Percentage
$\frac{1}{2}$	.50	50%
$\frac{1}{4}$	.25	25%
$\frac{1}{3}$	.33	
$\frac{1}{5}$	.20	20%
$\frac{2}{5}$	.40	40%
$\frac{2}{3}$	.66	66%

p. Juanita Perez, the owner of a small sporting goods store, purchased packages of pricing tickets at $15\frac{1}{2}$ cents for each package. How many packages of pricing tickets could Ms. Perez purchase for $7.50?

_____

q. Toys, Inc., had a sale on all merchandise during the months of January and February. Discount percentages ranged from 10 percent to 50 percent. Calculate the amount of discount on each item given below. Remember to round in favor of the business.

Item	Retail Price	Discount	Decimal Fraction	Discount Amount
Board game	$14.95	20%	.20	$
Toy gun	$8.00	50%	.50	$
Sled	$24.00	$33\frac{1}{3}\%$		$ 8.00
Coloring book	$0.79	15%		$ .12
Stuffed toy	$19.95	20%		$ .99
Electronic game	$49.95	40%	.40	$ 19.98

SECTION 2
ORDERING
AND RECEIVING
MERCHANDISE

Section 1 covered the basic math skills that are necessary for the field of marketing. In this and other sections, you will be using these skills for different marketing applications. Your ability to apply math skills to real-life situations will increase your chances of obtaining a good job. Once on the job, these skills will help you become a more valuable employee.

Before a business can sell merchandise, it must first have merchandise to sell. This section will explain the process of ordering and receiving merchandise. Study the terminology (words), ideas, and sample problems presented. Complete the problems at the end of the section. Successful completion of these problems will indicate that you understand the basics of ordering and receiving merchandise.

After completing this section, you will be able to:

1. Explain the process a business follows in ordering and receiving merchandise.

2. Explain the purpose and parts of a purchase order.

3. Check the accuracy of the extensions and the total on a purchase order.

4. Explain the purpose and parts of an invoice.

5. Compare the information on an invoice with the merchandise received.

6. Calculate the different types of discounts offered by manufacturers and distributors.

PROCESS OF ORDERING AND RECEIVING MERCHANDISE

Once merchandise is chosen, an order to purchase the items is prepared. This order is called a *purchase order* (also called a PO for short). A copy of the purchase order is sent to the manufacturer or distributor from whom the products are to be purchased. The manufacturer or distributor will then send the merchandise to the business that ordered the goods. A copy of the *invoice*, or *bill*, for the merchandise is also sent. Figure 2-1 shows a diagram of the process a business follows in ordering and receiving merchandise.

Figure 2-1
Process of Ordering and Receiving Merchandise

PURCHASE ORDER
TO:

The Fashion Place

A & A Designers
INVOICE

A AND A
APPAREL DESIGNERS, INC.

Merchandise is shipped by manufacturer

Illus. 2-1

Merchandise is delivered to a business from the manufacturer.

PURCHASE ORDERS

When merchandise is ordered, a purchase order is completed by the businessperson who orders the merchandise. A sample purchase order is shown in Figure 2-2. The various parts have been numbered and are explained immediately following the sample purchase order.

Figure 2-2
Purchase Order

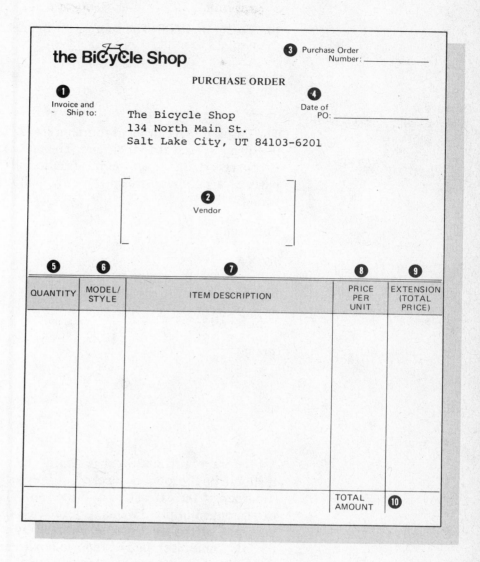

1. *Invoice and Ship to*—Name and address of the business ordering the merchandise.

2. *Vendor*—Name and address of the manufacturer or distributor from whom the goods were ordered.

3. *Purchase Order Number*—The number assigned to the purchase order by the business ordering the merchandise.

4. *Date of PO*—Date the purchase order is written by the business ordering the merchandise.

5. *Quantity*—The amount of each item of merchandise ordered.

6. *Model/Style*—A number and/or letter code that may stand for model, style, size, color, or other description of the item.

7. *Item Description*—The name of the item ordered, plus any special identification such as color, size, weight, etc.

8. *Price per Unit*—The price of each item of merchandise ordered.

9. *Extension*—Determined by multiplying the quantity times the price per unit.

10. *Total Amount*—The sum of all figures appearing in the extension column.

1 Learning Activity	The Fashion Place ordered fourteen size 3/5 dresses (style #163XA) for the spring season at $44.90 each. The purchase order was completed on February 12. Based on the information given, identify (by name) the parts of a purchase order where the following information would be found.

Fourteen   _____

163XA   _____

Size 3/5 dresses   _____

February 12   _____

$44.90   _____

Before a purchase order is sent to the manufacturer or distributor, it should be thoroughly checked. It is especially important to verify the accuracy of the extensions and the total. To check the accuracy of an extension, multiply the quantity ordered times the price per unit. The accuracy of the total can be checked by adding all extensions. If an error is found, it should be reported to a supervisor before the purchase order is mailed to the manufacturer or distributor. Examine the extensions and total amount calculated on the following purchase order.

Quantity	Model/ Style	Item Description	Unit Price	Extension (Total Price)
3	45-7	35 mm Cameras	$219.00	$657.00
2	37-9	35 mm Tripods	35.00	70.00
			Total Amount	$727.00

Illus. 2-2

To calculate extensions on a purchase order, multiply the quantity ordered times the price per unit.

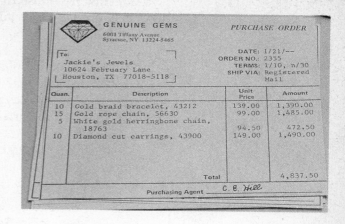

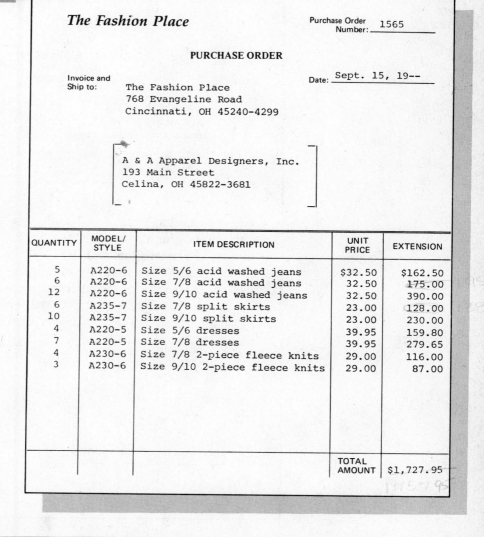

2
Learning Activity

Check the accuracy of the extensions and total amount on the purchase order below. Circle the incorrect numbers and write in the correct amount.

The Fashion Place

Purchase Order Number: 1565

PURCHASE ORDER

Invoice and Ship to:

The Fashion Place
768 Evangeline Road
Cincinnati, OH 45240-4299

Date: Sept. 15, 19--

A & A Apparel Designers, Inc.
193 Main Street
Celina, OH 45822-3681

QUANTITY	MODEL/STYLE	ITEM DESCRIPTION	UNIT PRICE	EXTENSION
5	A220-6	Size 5/6 acid washed jeans	$32.50	$162.50
6	A220-6	Size 7/8 acid washed jeans	32.50	175.00
12	A220-6	Size 9/10 acid washed jeans	32.50	390.00
6	A235-7	Size 7/8 split skirts	23.00	128.00
10	A235-7	Size 9/10 split skirts	23.00	230.00
4	A220-5	Size 5/6 dresses	39.95	159.80
7	A220-5	Size 7/8 dresses	39.95	279.65
4	A230-6	Size 7/8 2-piece fleece knits	29.00	116.00
3	A230-6	Size 9/10 2-piece fleece knits	29.00	87.00
			TOTAL AMOUNT	$1,727.95

INVOICES

When merchandise that has been ordered arrives at a business, an *invoice* (or *bill*) is usually sent with the merchandise. An invoice is an itemized list of goods shipped. It also usually shows the price of the merchandise and the terms of sale. A sample invoice is shown in Figure 2-3. Notice how similar an invoice is to a purchase order. Most of the information contained on the invoice, such as PO number, quantity, model/style, item description, price per unit, and extension are the same as found on the purchase order. The date on the invoice will be either the date the merchandise was shipped or the date the invoice was completed. Other information not found on the PO, such as terms, gross amount, discount, and net amount, will be explained in more detail later in this section.

Figure 2-3
Invoice

INVOICE

A AND A
APPAREL DESIGNERS, INC.
193 Main Street
Celina, OH 45822-3681

Date: _____

To: The Fashion Place   P.O. Number: _____
768 Evangeline Road
Cincinnati, OH 45240-4299   Terms: _____

Quantity	Model/ Style	Item Description	Price Per Unit	Extension (Total Price)

Gross Amount (Total) $ _____
Less Discount   _____
Net Amount $ _____

Checking the Accuracy of the Invoice

When an invoice comes with merchandise, follow the steps outlined below to receive and check the merchandise.

Step 1: Unpack the merchandise and check it for damage or spoilage. Any damage or spoilage should be noted on the invoice and brought to the attention of a supervisor.

Step 2: Before referring to the invoice, count the merchandise. After you count each item, place a check mark (✓) next to the quantity figure on the invoice if it agrees with your count.

Quantity	Model/ Style	Item Description	Unit Price	Extension
14✓	163XA	Size 3/5 dresses	$44.90	$628.60

Step 3: Check to make sure that the model/style number and the description of the merchandise agree with what is received. Place a check mark (✓) next to the model/style number if the two agree.

Quantity	Model/ Style	Item Description	Unit Price	Extension
14	163XA✓	Size 3/5 dresses	$44.90	$628.60

Step 4: Match the original purchase order with the invoice to make sure that the quantity and price shown on the invoice agree with the information on the purchase order. Place a check mark (✓) next to the unit price on the invoice to show that it has been compared to the purchase order.

Quantity	Model/ Style	Item Description	Unit Price	Extension
14	163XA	Size 3/5 dresses	$44.90✓	$628.60

Sometimes the manufacturer or distributor is unable to ship what was originally ordered. If this is the case, the missing item will still be listed on the invoice; but in place of the unit price an abbreviation such as BO (back order) or OS (out of stock) will be shown. *BO* means the merchandise will be shipped at a later date. *OS* means the merchandise is not in stock and will not be shipped.

Step 5: Math calculations on the invoice are referred to as *extensions*, and they must be checked for accuracy. These calculations are done exactly the same way as extensions on purchase orders: Multiply the quantity shipped times the unit price. After you check the accuracy of each extension, place a check mark (✓) after the figure in the extension column. If you find an

To check for accuracy, compare the information given on the invoice with the merchandise received.

incorrect extension, write the correct figure with a pencil on the invoice and bring this error to the attention of a supervisor.

Quantity	Model/ Style	Item Description	Unit Price	Extension
14	163XA	Size 3/5 dresses	$44.90	$628.60✓

$$14 \times \$44.90 = \$628.60$$

Step 6: Check the accuracy of the total amount shown at the bottom of the invoice. The total amount of the invoice is the sum of all extensions. This calculation is made by adding all extensions on the invoice. After you check the accuracy of the total, place a check mark (✓) next to the total amount. If the total is incorrect, write the correct figure in pencil and bring this error to the attention of a supervisor.

Quantity	Model/ Style	Item Description	Unit Price	Extension
14	163XA	Size 3/5 dresses	$44.90	$628.60
			Total Amount	$628.60✓

Step 7: After Steps 1-6 have been completed, the invoice is sent to the accounting office. Here it is processed for payment to the manufacturer or distributor.

3 Learning Activity

Explain in your own words the seven steps to follow in checking merchandise received against the invoice.

Step 1: open ups ✓ for damages. look at it

Step 2:

Step 3: ✓ model numbers, style numbers

Step 4: match original P.O. w/ invoice, ✓ prices

Step 5: make necessary extensions circle wrong numbers

Step 6: check accuracy

Step 7: send invoice over to ACCOUNTING

4
Learning Activity

Complete the extensions and totals on the following invoices.

Invoice 1

		INVOICE		
Quantity	Model/ Size	Item	Unit Price	Extension
10	16X-64"	Competition water skis	$105.00	
15	16X-66"	Competition water skis	110.00	
10	16X-70"	Competition water skis	115.00	
30	75 ft.	Single handle ski ropes	15.50	
20	100 ft.	Single handle ski ropes	17.50	
			Total Amount	

Invoice 2

		INVOICE		
Quantity	Size	Item	Unit Price	Extension
15	10M	Men's blue jogging shoes	$27.95	
12	10N	Men's blue jogging shoes	27.95	
10	10W	Men's blue jogging shoes	27.95	
10	8D	Men's brown leather boots	40.00	
15	$9\frac{1}{2}$C	Men's brown leather boots	40.00	
6	Pkgs.	Brown shoelaces	4.75	
			Total Amount	

Invoices and Units of Measure

Merchandise may be listed on invoices in dozen and gross lots. To compare the quantity received with the quantity shown on the invoice, these amounts must be converted (changed) to units or number of pieces. For example, if an invoice lists one gross of paper tablets, this means that there should be 144 pieces (tablets) in the shipment. Study the following conversions for a better understanding of the quantities you are likely to find listed on invoices.

$$1 \text{ dozen (doz)} = 12 \text{ pieces (pcs)}$$

$$1\tfrac{1}{2} \text{ dozen} = 18 \text{ pieces } (1\tfrac{1}{2} \times 12 = 18)$$

$$2 \text{ dozen} = 24 \text{ pieces } (2 \times 12 = 24)$$

$$1 \text{ gross} = 144 \text{ pieces}$$

$$1\tfrac{1}{2} \text{ gross} = 216 \text{ pieces } (1\tfrac{1}{2} \times 144 = 216)$$

$$1 \text{ gross} = 12 \text{ dozen}$$

$$1\tfrac{1}{2} \text{ gross} = 18 \text{ dozen } (1\tfrac{1}{2} \times 12 = 18)$$

5
Learning Activity

Using the conversions above, change the quantity shown to the unit specified.

a. 5 doz = _____ pcs

b. 2 gross = _____ pcs

c. $8\tfrac{1}{4}$ gross = _____ pcs

d. $\tfrac{1}{3}$ gross = _____ pcs

e. 5 gross = _____ doz

f. $4\tfrac{1}{3}$ doz = _____ pcs

g. 3 gross = _____ doz = _____ pcs

h. $\tfrac{1}{2}$ gross = _____ doz = _____ pcs

i. 12 gross = _____ doz = _____ pcs

j. $1\tfrac{3}{4}$ gross = _____ doz = _____ pcs

Weights and Measures Used in Ordering and Receiving Merchandise

Merchandise appearing on an invoice can be listed by size, weight, dimension, or liquid measure. You must be able to understand basic measurements to determine if the merchandise received was actually what was ordered.

The weights and measures table, Table 2-1, lists several types of measures that commonly appear on invoices.

Table 2-1
Weights and Measures Table

Weight	Dimension	Liquid Measure	Size
Pounds	Inches	Cups	Children's 3-6X
Grams	Centimeters	Pints	Children's 7-14
Kilograms	Feet	Quarts	Juniors 3-15
	Meters	Liters	Misses 6-18
	Yards	Gallons	Men's 36-50

Metric measurement is used increasingly in business today. It really is not difficult to use and understand. For example, if a business ordered men's belts and the invoice showed the lengths of these belts in centimeters, you would verify the length by the following simple procedure:

Step 1: Sort all belts by length, checking for defects. Put all identical sizes together.

Step 2: Use a meter stick or metric tape measure to measure only one belt of each size.

Step 3: Count the number of belts in each size and check the quantity shown on the invoice.

Quantity	Size	Item	Unit	Extension
10	81 cm	Brown Leather Belts	$6.50	$ 65.00
15	86 cm	" " "	6.75	101.25
20	92 cm	" " "	7.00	140.00
10	97 cm	" " "	7.25	72.50

Metric measurement is simple! Metric weight scales weigh in grams or kilograms. Meter sticks or metric tape measures show measurement in centimeters and meters. Liter measuring containers measure liquids.

6
Learning Activity

Describe the steps you would follow in checking merchandise that arrives with metric measurements of length.

Step 1:

Step 2:

Step 3:

TYPES OF DISCOUNTS OFFERED BY MANUFAC-TURERS AND DISTRIBUTORS

Manufacturers and distributors offer many different types of discounts to businesses. These discounts are designed to stimulate business and encourage prompt payment of bills.

A discount is actually a reduction in the price of the merchandise purchased by a business. The most common types of discounts offered businesses include:

1. Cash discounts
2. Trade discounts
3. Quantity discounts
4. Cumulative quantity discounts
5. Seasonal discounts
6. Promotional discounts

Cash Discounts

A *cash discount*, the most common type of discount, is that given to a business by manufacturers or distributors to insure that the invoice is paid within a specified period of time. This type of discount is deducted from the amount due after all other discounts, if any, have been subtracted. For example, if the total (gross) amount shown on an invoice is $1,000 and the cash discount is 5 percent, the net amount would be $950 ($1,000 × 0.05 = $50; $1,000 − $50 = $950). The cash discount is subtracted from the original amount to determine the amount due.

When determining a cash discount, it is often necessary to know the number of days in each month of the year. Refer to Table 2-2 for the correct number of days in each month.

Illus. 2-4

Most manufacturers and distributors offer some type of discount to businesses. If a grocery store places a large order, it may receive a quantity discount.

Table 2-2
Days in Each Month

January	31 days	July	31 days
February	28 or 29 days	August	31 days
March	31 days	September	30 days
April	30 days	October	31 days
May	31 days	November	30 days
June	30 days	December	31 days

The amount of the cash discount and the terms (credit terms) for payment appear next to the word *terms* on the top portion of the invoice. There are a number of common terms for payment with which you should become familiar. These include: ordinary, advanced, extra, EOM (end of month), and ROG (receipt of goods).

Ordinary Terms. The most common cash discount is called *ordinary terms*. An example would be 2/10, N30 or 2/10, net 30. This means that the business can deduct a 2 percent discount from the total amount shown if paid within 10 days of the date shown on the invoice.

For example, if the net amount appearing on an invoice is $300 and the date of the invoice is August 16, the 2 percent discount of $6.00 (0.02 × $300 = $6.00) could be deducted until August 26 (August 16 + 10 days).

If the 2 percent discount is not taken by August 26, then the $300 net amount of the invoice would be payable by September 15. This date is determined by adding 30 days to the August 16 date. (31 days in August − 16 days = 15 days in August; 30 days = 15 days in August + 15 days in September; August 16 + 30 days = September 15.)

Invoice date: August 16

Terms: 2/10, N30

Number of days 2 percent discount can be taken: 10 days

Deadline for taking discount: August 16 + 10 days = August 26

Deadline for paying net amount: August 16 + 30 days = September 15

Amount of discount: 2% × $300 = 0.02 × $300 = $6.00

Amount payable on or before August 26: $300 − $6.00 = $294.00

Amount payable from August 27 to September 15: $300

7
Learning Activity

The cash discount terms appearing on an invoice are 3/15, N30. The invoice is dated April 1 for a net amount of $500. Determine the following.

Deadline for taking discount _____

Discount amount $_____

Amount payable if discount is taken $_____

Deadline date for paying net amount _____

Advanced Terms. When *advanced terms* are granted, the discount period is based on a date later than the actual date of the invoice. This type of cash discount is offered to encourage businesses to buy earlier. An example of advanced terms might be 3/10, N30, as of April 1 on an invoice dated March 1. Advanced terms are figured in the same way as ordinary terms except that the discount period begins on the stated discount date rather than on the actual invoice date.

For example, if a $1,600 invoice had terms of 3/10, N30, as of April 1, the 3 percent discount of $48.00 could be taken until April 11 (April 1 + 10 days = April 11). The net amount of the invoice ($1,600) would be payable by May 1 (April 1 + 30 days = May 1).

8
Learning Activity

The cash discount terms on an invoice are 4/10, net 45, as of December 1. The invoice is dated October 12 for a net amount of $2,500. Determine the following.

Deadline for taking discount _____

Discount amount $_____

Amount payable if discount is taken $_____

Deadline for paying net amount _____

Extra Terms. Under *extra terms*, extra time is allowed for deducting the cash discount. An example of extra terms is 3/10, N30, 30 extra. This gives the business 40 days (30 extra + 10 ordinary) to take advantage of the 3 percent discount. The terms of 3/10, N30 apply after the 30 days extra time period has ended.

For example, if the terms are 3/10, N30, 30 extra, and the net amount is $200 on an invoice dated April 1, the discount of $6.00 could be taken until May 11 (April 1 + 40 days = May 11). The net amount would be payable by May 31 (April 1 + 30 days extra = May 1 + 30 days = May 31).

9
Learning Activity

The cash discount terms appearing on an invoice are 2/10, net 30, 40 extra. The invoice is dated May 3 for a net amount of $3,000. Determine the following.

Deadline for taking discount _____

Discount amount $_____

Amount payable if discount is taken $_____

Deadline for paying net amount _____

EOM (End of Month) Terms. Under *EOM terms*, the time for payment begins at the end of the month shown as the invoice date. (When EOM terms are used, invoices dated after the 25th of the month are considered to fall in the following month.)

An example of EOM terms might be 2/10, N30, EOM. If the invoice amount is $2,000, and the date on the invoice is November 15, the 2 percent discount of $40.00 could be taken until December 10 (10 days after the beginning of the next month). If the discount is not taken, the net amount of $2,000 would be payable December 30.

---

10 Learning Activity

The cash discount terms appearing on an invoice are 5/15, N30, EOM. The invoice is dated June 28 for a net amount of $750. Determine the following.

Deadline for taking discount _____

Discount amount $_____

Amount payable if discount is taken $_____

Deadline for paying net amount _____

ROG (Receipt of Goods) Terms. Under *ROG terms*, the discount period begins when the merchandise is received by the purchaser. The invoice date itself is not taken into consideration. An example of ROG terms would be 3/10, net 30, ROG. If the invoice is dated November 12, the amount is $1,500, and the goods are received by the purchaser on November 21, the 3 percent discount of $45.00 could be taken until December 1 (November 21 + 10 days = December 1). The net amount would be payable 30 days after the merchandise is received, or on December 21 (November 21 + 30 days = December 21). Remember, use the date of receipt, *not* the date of the invoice, as the basis of the discount period for ROG terms.

---

11 Learning Activity

The cash discount terms appearing on an invoice are 4/20, net 30, ROG. The invoice is dated September 1 for a net amount of $3,200. The merchandise was received November 28. Determine the following.

Deadline for taking discount _____

Discount amount $_____

Amount payable if discount is taken $_____

Deadline for paying net amount _____

Trade Discounts

A *trade discount* is usually not a price reduction, but rather a method of price quoting based on suggested retail prices (or list prices). The *suggested retail price* is established by manufacturers or distributors to help businesses determine the proper retail price to charge for merchandise. This price must be large enough to cover business expenses and yet return a fair profit.

If a manufacturer quoted the price for a lawn mower at $150.00 less 40 percent, the cost to the business would be $90.00. This figure is arrived at in the following manner.

Step 1: Change the 40 percent to a decimal fraction of 0.40.

Step 2: Multiply the $150.00 × 0.40. This equals $60.00, which is the trade discount.

Step 3: Subtract the trade discount ($60.00) from the retail price ($150.00). The result is the cost of the lawn mower to the business. This figure is known as the *net cost*.

12
Learning Activity

Calculate the trade discount and actual (net) cost for each invoice total shown below.

Amount of Purchase	Trade Discount	Amount of Discount	Net Cost to Business
$1,800	40%	$ 720	$ 1090
$5,000	$33\frac{1}{3}$%	$ 1667	$
$2,250	50%	$ 1125	$ 1125
$3,000	$66\frac{2}{3}$%	$ 2000	$ 1000
$7,500	45%	$ 3375	$ 4125

Quantity Discounts

It is usually less expensive for a manufacturer or distributor to deliver large quantities of a product to the purchaser. To encourage the purchase of large quantities, a *quantity discount* may be offered. A typical price list might show quantity discounts as follows:

Quantity Price List

Item	1-6	7-12	13-24	25-48	49-96	97 or More
75W light bulbs	$0.34 ea	$0.33 ea	$0.32 ea	$0.30 ea	$0.29 ea	$0.27 ea

If an order was placed for thirty-six 75W light bulbs, the cost would be:

$$36 \times \$0.30 = \$10.80$$

<table>
<tr><td>

13

Learning Activity

</td><td>

Using the quantity price list above, calculate the cost of an order of seventy-two 75W light bulbs.

_____ × $_____ = $_____

</td></tr>
</table>

Cumulative Quantity Discounts

Cumulative quantity discounts are discounts given to businesses that have purchased at least a certain dollar amount during a given period of time. For example, a shoe manufacturing company may allow a 2 percent cumulative discount for purchases totaling more than $1,000 in 30 days. If a shoe store bought $1,800 worth of shoes from the manufacturer between January 15 and February 14, the shoe store could deduct 2 percent of $1,800, or $36.00. This would mean that the shoe store would pay $1,764 for the shoes instead of the original $1,800.

<table>
<tr><td>

14

Learning Activity

</td><td>

Calculate the cumulative quantity discounts given below.

Amount of Purchases	Minimum Purchase	Cumulative Quantity Discount	Amount of Discount	Net Cost to Business
$2,600	$2,000	$1\frac{1}{2}\%$	$_____	$_____
$1,500	$1,000	2%	$_____	$_____
$2,400	$2,000	$\frac{3}{4}\%$	$_____	$_____
$1,000	$2,000	3%	$_____	$_____
$5,500	$5,000	$\frac{1}{2}\%$	$_____	$_____
$3,200	$3,000	$1\frac{1}{4}\%$	$_____	$_____
$1,200	$1,500	$2\frac{1}{2}\%$	$_____	$_____
$900	$1,000	4%	$_____	$_____

</td></tr>
</table>

Seasonal Discounts

Seasonal discounts are discounts allowed when merchandise is purchased long before the season for the products. For example, discounts are allowed:

1. On lawn mowers purchased before February 15
2. On Halloween costumes purchased before July 31
3. On Christmas decorations purchased before September 10
4. On water skis purchased before January 31

A seasonal discount is calculated just like a cumulative quantity discount—by multiplying the amount of the purchase times the percent of discount.

Illus. 2-5

Seasonal discounts may be passed on to customers of the store. Thus, people who buy lawn equipment in the winter can often get a better price.

15 Learning Activity

Calculate the seasonal discounts given below.

Item	Amount of Purchase	Seasonal Discount	Amount of Discount	Net Cost to Business
Lawn mowers	$1,220.00	15%	$	$
Halloween costumes	$327.00	5%	$ 16.35	$ 310.65
Christmas decorations	$625.00	20%	$	$
Water skis	$1,757.00	10%	$	$ 1,581.30

Promotional Discounts

Promotional discounts are given to businesses that agree to advertise a product, place the product on preferred shelf space or store location, or otherwise actively promote the product. By offering promotional discounts, the manufacturer or distributor hopes to increase retail customer demand for the product.

A promotional discount, if stated as a percentage, is calculated exactly the same as a cumulative quantity discount or a seasonal discount. Many times promotional discounts are given in dollar amounts. You may then be asked to determine the percentage of the promotional discount. For example, a manufacturer or distributor may offer a $200 promotional discount on purchases of camping equipment totaling $2,000. The net amount payable by the business ($1,800) is determined by subtracting the $200 discount from the total purchase price of $2,000. The percentage of the promotional discount (10 percent) is found by dividing the promotional discount amount ($200) by the total purchase price of $2,000.

$$\begin{array}{r} \$2,000 \\ -\ 200 \\ \hline \$1,800 \end{array} \qquad \qquad 2{,}000\overline{)\begin{array}{l} 0.1 = 10\% \\ 200.0 \\ \underline{200\ 0} \end{array}}$$

16
Learning Activity

Determine the percent of discount and the total due if the following promotional discounts are taken.

Item	Amount of Purchase	Promotional Discount	Net Cost to Business	Discount
Motorcycles	$5,250	$420.00	$	%
Ski boots	$1,200	$120.00	$	%
Tennis rackets	$1,750	$87.50	$	%
Sailboats	$12,390	$185.85	$	%

SECTION 2
USING MATH IN MARKETING

1. Explain the purpose of a purchase order.

Once merchandise is chosen an order to
purchase the item is prepared.

2. Describe the following parts of a purchase order.

  a. Vendor

name and address of manufacturer or
distributor

  b. Quantity

the number of each item of merchandise
ordered.

  c. Model/Style

  d. Item Description

what is ordered.

  e. Purchase Order Number

number of the purchase order

  f. Date of PO

Date the purchase order is written

  g. Price per Unit

price or cost/unit of merchandise order

  h. Extension

multiply the quantity times the price per
unit.

3. Explain the difference between a purchase order and an invoice.

Purchase order - an order to purchase

Invoice - name & address of business

4. Calculate the extensions and total on the purchase order shown below.

state hardware store

Purchase Order Number: 1312

PURCHASE ORDER

Invoice and Ship to:

State Hardware Store
157 S. Main St.
Cedar City, UT 84720-0375

Date of PO: Jan. 5, 19--

Intercity Supply Corp.
4576 Redwood Road
Sacramento, CA 95815-5597

QUANTITY	MODEL/ STYLE	ITEM DESCRIPTION	UNIT PRICE	EXTENSION
15	9K-324	$6\frac{1}{2}$" Tungsten saw blades	$ 6.50	
8	9K-327	7" Tungsten saw blades	10.75	
3	9K-173	$1\frac{1}{2}$ HP Router	77.25	
10	9K-108	7", $1\frac{2}{3}$ HP saw	32.85	
5	9K-118	$7\frac{1}{2}$", $2\frac{1}{8}$ HP saw	85.00	
10	9K-171	$\frac{1}{2}$ HP Sabre saw	9.95	
4	9K-172	$\frac{3}{8}$ HP Power planer	42.85	
8	9K-105	$\frac{3}{8}$" Variable speed drill	28.88	
6	9K-116	$\frac{1}{2}$ HP Dual-action pad sander	41.25	
			TOTAL AMOUNT	

5. Explain the seven steps to be followed in checking merchandise received against the invoice.

Step 1: unpack merchandise, check for damages

Step 2: count the merchandise

Step 3: make sure the model/style number matches w/what you received

Name _____

Step 4: match the original purchase orders w/ the invoice

Step 5: math calculations on the invoice are referred to as extensions

Step 6: check accuracy of the total amount

Step 7: invoice is sent to accounting office and scheduled for payment

6. Complete the extensions and total (gross amount) on the following two invoices.

Invoice A

INVOICE

MIDWEST
MANUFACTURING COMPANY
Jackson, MI 49201-1773

To: Farnsworth's
156 Oak Harbor Road
Battle Creek, MI 49017-4200

Date: February 8,19--
P.O. Number: 3567
Terms: 3/15 N30 as of April 1

Quantity	Size	Item Description	Unit Price	Extension
27	32" 29"	Stonewash jeans	$12.88	347.76
21	34" 31"	Stonewash jeans	12.88	270.48
15	36" 32"	Stonewash jeans	12.88	193.20
18	42-44L	Crew neck sweaters	13.67	246.06
15	34-36S	Crew neck sweaters	13.67	205.05
12	38-40M	Crew neck sweaters	13.67	164.04
16	29" 29"	Twill pants	11.75	188.—
15	31" 30"	Twill pants	11.75	176.25
12	33" 31"	Twill pants	11.75	141.—
10	34" 32"	Twill pants	11.75	117.50

Gross Amount (Total) $ 2049.34
Less Discount _____
Net Amount $ _____

Ordering and Receiving Merchandise   67

Invoice B

INVOICE

Modern PAINT SUPPLY

Toledo, OH 43612-9761

		Date: April 4, 19--
To:	Kidman's Hardware	P.O. Number: 1765
	635 Main St.	Terms: 2/10, N30
	Norwalk, OH 44857-4538	

Quantity	Color Number	Item Description	Unit Price	Extension
15 Gal	30-K-33	Interior white acrylic latex paint	$9.49	
5 Gal	30-K-32	Interior ivory acrylic latex paint	9.49	
10 Gal	30-K-31	Interior pebble beige acrylic latex paint	9.49	
17 Gal	30-K-23	White exterior latex paint	4.89	
8 Gal	30-K-27	Apache gold exterior latex paint	4.89	
10 Gal	30-K-89	White oil base primer	5.70	
5 Gal	30-K-56	Water proofing paint	9.00	
10 Gal	30-K-53	Pewter gray latex floor paint	5.15	

Gross Amount (Total) $ _____

Less Discount _____

Net Amount $ _____

7. Using the conversion table given in this section, change the following to number of pieces.

a. 7 dozen = _____ pcs

b. $10\frac{1}{2}$ gross = _____ pcs

c. 2 gross = _____ doz = _____ pcs

d. $6\frac{1}{4}$ dozen = _____ pcs

e. 3 gross = _____ pcs

f. $\frac{1}{4}$ gross = _____ doz = _____ pcs

g. $2\frac{3}{4}$ gross = _____ pcs

h. 8 dozen = _____ pcs

Name _____

8. Describe the three steps to be followed in checking the receipt of merchandise that arrives with metric measurements of length.

Step 1: sort all belts by length

Step 2: use a meter stick or metric tape

Step 3: count the number and size

9. The cash discount terms appearing on an invoice are 6/10, N45. The invoice is dated October 23 for a net amount of $2,650. Determine the following.

a. Deadline date for taking discount   November 2

b. Discount amount $ 159

c. Amount payable if discount is taken $ 2,491

d. Deadline date for paying net amount   December 7

e. Amount saved by taking advantage of the discount $ 159

10. The cash discount terms appearing on an invoice are 5/10, net 30, as of June 15. The invoice is dated May 27 for a net amount of $750. Determine the following.

a. Deadline date for taking discount   June 25

b. Discount amount $ 7.50

c. Amount payable if discount is taken $ 1250

d. Deadline for paying net amount   July 15

11. The cash discount terms appearing on an invoice are 3/15, N45, 40 extra. The invoice is dated January 12 for a net amount of $6,000. Determine the following.

a. Deadline date for taking discount   march 8

b. Discount amount $ 180

c. Amount payable if discount is taken $ 5820

d. Deadline date for paying net amount   April 7

12. The cash discount terms appearing on an invoice are 7/10, net 30, EOM. The invoice is dated August 26 for a net amount of $1,230. Determine the following.

a. Deadline date for taking discount _____

b. Discount amount $_____

c. Amount payable if discount is taken $_____

d. Deadline for paying net amount _____

13. The cash terms applying on an invoice are 3/15, N30, ROG. The invoice is dated September 15 for a net amount of $7,100. The merchandise was received on October 17. Determine the following.

a. Deadline date for taking discount _____

b. Discount amount $_____

c. Amount payable if discount is taken $_____

d. Deadline for paying net amount _____

14. What do the following abbreviations stand for?

a. ROG _____

b. EOM _____

15. Determine the cash discount date and the amount payable if the invoice is paid on or before the discount date.

	Amount of Invoice	Date of Invoice	Terms	Date of Delivery	Cash Discount Date	Amount Payable
a.	$1,350.00	March 5	2/15, 90 extra	March 10	_____	$_____
b.	$76.80	July 1	3/10, N30, EOM	July 12	_____	$_____
c.	$625.80	June 15	5/10, net 60	August 20	_____	$_____
d.	$985.00	February 13	4/15, N30, ROG	April 28	_____	$_____
e.	$4,675.00	October 12	3/10, N30, as of November 30	November 1	_____	$_____
f.	$417.25	March 24	5/15, net 30, 30 extra	April 5	_____	$_____
g.	$1,235.76	December 1	3/10, N30, EOM, ROG	February 10	_____	$_____

Name _____

16. Calculate the trade discounts and the actual (net) costs for the following invoice totals.

	Amount of Purchase	Trade Discount	Amount of Discount	Net Amount Due
a.	$1,680	30%	$	$ 1,176
b.	$4,375	$33\frac{1}{3}$%	$ 1,458.33	$ 2,916.67
c.	$2,936	50%	$	$
d.	$6,300	47%	$	$
e.	$2,920	40%	$	$
f.	$1,162	60%	$ 697.20	$ 464.80

17. A manufacturer's catalog shows the following quantity discounts for lipstick.

			Quantity		
Item	1-4	5-9	10-19	20-29	30 or More
Lipstick	$1.29 ea	$1.13 ea	$1.02 ea	$0.98 ea	$0.90 ea

Find the cost per unit and the total cost for a business ordering the following different quantities.

	Ordered	Cost per Unit	Total Cost
a.	2	$ 1.29	$ 2.58
b.	9	$ 1.13	$ 10.17
c.	7	$ 1.13	$ 7.91
d.	11	$ 1.02	$ 11.22
e.	18	$ 1.02	$ 18.26
f.	24	$ .98	$ 23.52
g.	29	$ .98	$ 28.42
h.	31	$ .90	$ 27.90
i.	75	$ .90	$ 67.50

18. A seasonal discount of 15 percent is given for purchases of bathing suits before February 10. A business purchases 155 women's bathing suits for $15.00 each. Determine the following.

    a. Total cost of the bathing suits without the seasonal discount $_____

    b. Actual cost of the bathing suits if purchased on February 1 $_____

    c. How much money could the business save by ordering the suits before February 10? $_____

    d. What will each suit cost if ordered on February 7? $_____

19. A business purchased $42,390 worth of merchandise during a four-month time period. The manufacturer allows a 7 percent cumulative quantity discount on purchases over $40,000 made in a six-month period. Determine the following.

    a. The amount of discount the business will receive $_____

    b. The total net amount the business must pay the manufacturer $_____

20. A business purchased motorcycles valued at $12,500 for the spring season. The manufacturer provided the business with a $250 promotional discount. Determine the following.

    a. Total amount payable by business $_____

    b. Percentage of discount $250 represents   _____%

SECTION 3
PRICING
MERCHANDISE

Once merchandise is received by a business, it must be properly priced for resale. In this section you will study the importance of pricing and the methods used in pricing merchandise. You will also learn how to calculate markdowns on merchandise.

After completing this section, you will be able to:

1. Explain the importance of proper pricing.
2. Explain the terms that are used in pricing.
3. Use basic markup formulas in pricing.
4. Calculate the initial markup as a percentage of cost or retail.
5. Calculate the retail price of merchandise using the cost method.
6. Calculate the retail price of merchandise using the retail method.
7. Calculate markdowns on merchandise.
8. Calculate the maintained markup as a percentage of cost.
9. Calculate unit selling prices and prices for fractional quantities.
10. Calculate the break-even point used by manufacturers in pricing products.

IMPORTANCE OF PROPER PRICING

People enter business to earn an income from the efforts they make and the risks they take. Earning an income in business is directly related to the proper pricing of merchandise. If a business does not charge enough for its merchandise, it will lose money. If it charges too much, the merchandise may not sell, and the business may not succeed. Every product sold must not only provide its individual share of the profit but must also cover its share of business expenses.

PRICING TERMINOLOGY

Before you can understand pricing, you must become familiar with the terminology used. Study the following explanation of terms for a better understanding of pricing.

1. *Retail Price*—The price at which merchandise is offered to the customer.
2. *Selling Price*—The price at which merchandise is actually sold.
3. *Cost Price* or *Cost*—The cost of merchandise paid by the business to a wholesaler or manufacturer.
4. *Initial Markup*—The difference between the original retail price and the cost of merchandise.
5. *Markdown*—The amount that merchandise is marked down (reduced) from the retail price.
6. *Maintained Markup*—The difference between the selling price and the cost of merchandise.

BASIC MARKUP FORMULAS

The preceding terms will be easier to understand if you carefully look over the markup formulas below. Then notice how these terms are used in the examples.

1. Cost + Initial Markup = *Retail Price*
2. Retail Price − Cost = *Initial Markup*
3. Retail Price − Initial Markup = *Cost*

Example 1: A pair of jeans costs a business $14.00. The jeans have an initial markup of $10.00. Determine the retail price.

Solution: Cost + Initial Markup = Retail Price

$14.00 + $10.00 = $24.00

Example 2: A shirt costs a business $9.00. The retail price of each shirt is $16.50. Determine the initial markup.

Solution: Retail Price − Cost = Initial Markup

$16.50 − $9.00 = $7.50

Example 3: The retail price for a pair of skis is $280.00. The initial markup is $125.00. Determine the cost.

Solution: Retail Price − Initial Markup = Cost

$280.00 − $125.00 = $155.00

1. A microwave oven costs a business $250.00. The initial markup is $125.00. Determine the retail price.

Retail Price $_____

2. A pair of shoes costs a business $20.00. The retail price is $35.00. Determine the initial markup.

Initial Markup $_____

3. The retail price for a leather coat is $129.00. The initial markup is $45.00. Determine the cost.

Cost $_____

MARKUP AS A PERCENTAGE OF COST OR RETAIL

Markup can be expressed as a percentage of the cost price or as a percentage of the retail price. Because you will be using these percentages later in this section, it is important for you to know how to calculate them.

Initial Markup as a Percentage of Cost

Initial markup as a percentage of cost is found by dividing the initial markup by the cost. For example, if an item costs $12.00 and has an initial markup of $8.00, the initial markup as a percentage of cost would be 67 percent, rounded to the nearest whole percent.

$$\text{IM\% (cost)} = \frac{\text{Initial Markup}}{\text{Cost}} = \frac{\$8.00}{\$12.00} = 0.66\frac{2}{3} = 66\frac{2}{3}\% = 67\%$$

2
Learning Activity

The cost of a leather coat is $120.00. The initial markup is $65.00. Determine the initial markup percentage based on cost.

Initial Markup % (cost) ____54____ %

Initial Markup as a Percentage of Retail

Initial markup as a percentage of retail is found by dividing the initial markup by the retail price. If an item costs $12.00 and has an initial markup of $8.00, the retail price would be $20.00. Markup as a percentage of retail would be 40 percent.

$$\text{IM\% (retail)} = \frac{\text{Initial Markup}}{\text{Retail}} = \frac{\$8.00}{\$20.00} = 0.40 = 40\%$$

3
Learning Activity

The cost of a leather coat is $120.00. The initial markup is $65.00. Determine the retail price and the initial markup percentage (rounded) based on retail.

Retail Price $___19500___

Initial Markup % (retail) ____5____ %

Even though the *dollar amount* of markup is the same in both of the previous examples, the *percentage* of markup is different depending on the method used (cost or retail).

CALCULATING THE RETAIL PRICE

There are two methods of pricing merchandise when the markup percentage and cost are known—the cost method and the retail method. Both are designed to insure that the business charges enough for its merchandise to cover operating expenses and to make a satisfactory net profit. Knowledge of both is important in determining the proper price at which merchandise should be sold.

Cost Method

Some small businesses prefer to calculate and express markup as a percentage of the cost of merchandise. This is the *cost method*. To use this method, change the markup percentage to a decimal and multiply by the cost of the merchandise. The retail price is the sum of the result of this calculation and the cost price. Expressed as a formula, this would read:

$$\text{Retail Price (cost method)} = (\text{Cost} \times \text{Markup \%}) + \text{Cost}$$

Example: If the cost price of a suit is $110.00 and the initial markup is 40 percent, the retail price using the cost method would be determined as follows.

$$\text{Retail Price} = (\text{Cost} \times \text{Markup \%}) + \text{Cost}$$
$$\text{Retail Price} = (\$110.00 \times 0.40) + \$110.00$$
$$\text{Retail Price} = \$44.00 + \$110.00$$
$$\text{Retail Price} = \$154.00$$

4
Learning Activity

The cost price of a compact disc player is $145.00. The suggested initial markup is $33\frac{1}{3}$ percent. Determine the retail price using the cost method.

Retail Price (cost method) $ _____

Retail Method

Because most businesses keep all of their records in terms of retail or sales dollars, the *retail method* of marking up merchandise is most widely used. In this method, the initial markup is expressed as a percentage of the unknown retail price. (The cost is known, but the initial markup is based on retail, not on cost.) Expressed as a formula, this would read:

$$\text{Retail Price (retail method)} = \frac{\text{Cost}}{100\% - \text{Markup \%}}$$

Example: If the cost of a suit is $110.00 and the initial markup percentage desired is 40 percent, the retail price using the retail method would be determined as follows.

$$\text{Retail Price} = \frac{\text{Cost}}{100\% - \text{Markup \%}}$$
$$\text{Retail Price} = \frac{\$110.00}{100\% - 40\%}$$
$$\text{Retail Price} = \frac{\$110.00}{0.60}$$
$$\text{Retail Price} = \$183.33$$

5
Learning Activity

The cost price of a compact disc player is $145.00. The suggested initial markup is $33\frac{1}{3}$ percent. Determine the retail price using the retail method.

Retail Price (retail method) $_____

Businesses must also know what they can afford to pay for merchandise. Once the initial markup percentage has been decided, the formula (a version of the formula given above) for finding the cost is:

$$Cost = Retail\ Price \times (100\% - Markup\ \%)$$

Example: If a business planned to sell lawn mowers for $160.00 retail each with a 50 percent markup, the cost the business could afford to pay for the lawn mowers would be determined as follows.

$$Cost = Retail\ Price \times (100\% - Markup\ \%)$$
$$Cost = \$160.00 \times (100\% - 50\%)$$
$$Cost = \$160.00 \times (0.50)$$
$$Cost = \$80.00$$

6
Learning Activity

A business plans to sell jeans for $19.95 retail, using a 48 percent markup. Determine the cost price the business could afford to pay for the jeans.

Cost Price $_____

Initial Markup Equivalents Table

If you found it difficult to use the markup formula given above $\left(Retail\ Price = \dfrac{Cost}{100\% - Markup\ \%}\right)$, you may find it easier to use an initial markup equivalents table, such as Table 3-1. This table lists initial markup percent based on cost and the equivalent initial markup percent based on retail. To use this table, find the desired markup based on retail in the left column. Then multiply the cost of the article by the percentage given in the right column. The result of this calculation added to the original cost price will be the same as the retail price using the retail method.

Table 3-1
Initial Markup Equivalents

Markup On Retail	Markup On Cost	Markup On Retail	Markup On Cost
4.8%	5.0%	25.0%	33.3%
5.0	5.3	26.0	35.0
6.0	6.4	27.0	37.0
7.0	7.5	27.3	37.5
8.0	8.7	28.0	39.0
9.0	10.0	28.5	40.0
10.0	11.1	29.0	40.9
10.7	12.0	30.0	42.9
11.0	12.4	31.0	45.0
11.1	12.5	32.0	47.1
12.0	13.6	33.3	50.0
12.5	14.3	34.0	51.5
13.0	15.0	35.0	53.9
14.0	16.3	35.5	55.0
15.0	17.7	36.0	56.3
16.0	19.1	37.0	58.8
16.7	20.0	37.5	60.0
17.0	20.5	38.0	61.3
17.5	21.2	39.0	64.0
18.0	22.0	39.5	65.5
18.5	22.7	40.0	66.7
19.0	23.5	41.0	70.0
20.0	25.0	42.0	72.4
21.0	26.6	42.8	75.0
22.0	28.2	44.4	80.0
22.5	29.0	46.1	85.0
23.0	29.9	47.5	90.0
23.1	30.0	48.7	95.0
24.0	31.6	50.0	100.0

7
Learning Activity

A clock radio with telephone costs a business $40.00. The suggested initial markup based on retail is $37\frac{1}{2}$ percent. Find the retail price using Table 3-1.

Retail Price (retail method) $_____

MARKDOWNS

Many times, to reduce the quantity of merchandise on hand, a business will mark down merchandise by a certain percentage. This reduction is always based on the retail price of the merchandise. For example, to

Illus. 3-1

To reduce the quantity of merchandise on hand, a business may mark down merchandise by a certain percentage.

mark down by 25 percent the price of a pair of jeans that retailed at $20.00, a business would proceed as follows.

$$\text{Retail Price} \times \text{\% Markdown} = \text{\$ Reduction}$$
$$\$20.00 \times 0.25 = \$5.00$$

$$\text{Retail Price} - \text{\$ Reduction} = \text{Sales Price}$$
$$\$20.00 - \$5.00 = \$15.00$$

8
Learning Activity

A sport coat originally had a $105.00 retail price. The business decided to reduce the price on all sport coats by 30 percent. Determine the sale price.

Sale Price $_____

105.
x 30
31.50

105
73.50

Maintained Markup

When a business marks down merchandise, its original profit expectations are reduced. *Maintained markup* is the dollar markup actually realized on the sale. For example, suppose a product was originally retailed for $12.00 with an initial markup of $5.00. If it was then marked down 25 percent and sold for $9.00, the maintained markup would be $2.00. Expressed as a formula this would be:

$$\text{Maintained Markup} = \text{Sale Price} - \text{Cost}$$
$$\text{Maintained Markup} = \$9.00 - \$7.00 = \$2.00$$

9
Learning Activity

A billfold that originally cost a business $7.50 retailed for $15.00. Later the billfold was marked down 20 percent. Determine the maintained markup.

Maintained Markup $_____

The maintained markup can also be expressed as a percentage. For example, if a product costs $10.00, was originally priced at $15.00, and is now marked down $3.00, the maintained markup percentage is 16.7 percent. This figure is obtained by using the following formula.

$$\% \text{ of Maintained Markup} = \frac{\text{Maintained Markup (SP} - \text{Cost)}}{\text{Original Retail Price} - \text{Markdown in Dollars}}$$

$$\% \text{ of Maintained Markup} = \frac{\$2.00}{\$15.00 - \$3.00} = \frac{\$2.00}{\$12.00} = 0.167 = 16.7\%$$

10
Learning Activity

A calculator that cost a business $15.00 originally sold for $27.50 and is now marked down $9.50. Determine the maintained markup percentage.

Percent Maintained Markup   _____%

Determining Unit Selling Prices

Merchandise is often sold in a quantity of two or more units of an item. For example, soup may sell at 3 cans for $1.57. (The symbol @ means at.) To find the selling price for one unit (one can) you must divide the price ($1.57) by the number of units and round the answer up to the next whole cent. Thus, the customer buying the soup would pay 53¢ for one can:

$$\$1.57 \div 3 = 52\tfrac{1}{3}¢ \text{ or } 53¢$$

11
Learning Activity

Determine the price of one item given the following units and price per unit.

Item	Quantity		Price	Price of One Item (Unit)
Toothpaste	2 tubes	@	$2.79	$_____ per tube
Soap	5 bars	@	$1.65	$_____ per bar
Notebooks	box of 3 dozen	@	$21.24	$_____ per notebook
Videotapes	2 tapes	@	$5.00	$_____ per tape
Batteries	3 packages	@	$5.00	$_____ per package
Film	2 rolls	@	$7.54	$_____ per roll

Determining Prices for Fractional Quantities

Many times customers will buy a fractional part of an item or unit. For example, a customer may wish to buy $\frac{1}{2}$ yard of fabric that sells for $1.29 per yard. To determine the price to charge for $\frac{1}{2}$ yard, multiply the $1.29 by $\frac{1}{2}$. This calculation is shown below.

$$\$1.29 \times \frac{1}{2} = \frac{\$1.29}{2} = 64\frac{1}{2}\text{¢ or 65¢}$$

12
Learning Activity

Find the price for each fractional quantity given below.

Number Desired	Price per Unit	Price for Fractional Quantity
$\frac{1}{2}$ dozen eggs	89¢/dozen	_____¢
$\frac{1}{2}$ gallon punch	$2.29/gallon	$_____
$\frac{3}{4}$ pound hamburger	$1.88/pound	$_____
$\frac{1}{4}$ pound butter	$1.29/pound	_____¢
2 pieces pizza	$5.95/pizza (8 pcs)	$_____

You may also be asked to find the unit price of an item when you are given the price for a fractional quantity of that item. For example, to find the price of a one-pound box of raisins when a five-ounce package costs 49¢, divide the 49¢ by $\frac{5}{16}$ (16 ounces per pound).

$$\$0.49 \div \frac{5}{16} = \$0.49 \times \frac{16}{5} = \frac{\$7.84}{5} = \$1.57 \text{ per pound}$$

13
Learning Activity

Find the unit price for the following items.

Item and Price	Price/Unit
8-oz package of peanuts for $1.09	$_____ per pound
5 grapefruit for $1.00	$_____ per dozen
6 cans of baby food for $1.89	$_____ per case (24 cans/case)
3 pounds of cheese for $6.87	$_____ per loaf (5 pounds/loaf)
1 apple for $0.29	$_____ per dozen

PRICING BY PRODUCERS— BREAK-EVEN ANALYSIS

Companies that manufacture or produce products frequently use a process called *break-even analysis* to determine an appropriate price to charge for the products they produce. The *break-even point (BEP)* is the point where income from sales (price × quantity sold) equals the cost of producing the product. At the break-even point, the company shows no profit and no loss—it simply breaks even. If more units of the product are sold at the same price, the break-even point is exceeded and the business makes a profit. If fewer units are sold (less than the BEP), the business does not make a profit at this selling price.

To determine the break-even point, a business must first determine its fixed costs and its variable costs. *Fixed costs* do not go up or down as the level of production goes up or down. Fixed costs include such items as rent, insurance, and equipment. The costs for equipment, for example, will not increase simply because production has gone up a certain number of units. On the other hand, *variable costs* go up or down in direct relationship to the level of production. Examples of variable costs include raw materials costs, production labor costs, and packaging. These costs will increase as production increases.

The per unit variable costs and selling price are used to determine the variable-cost margin. Then the break-even point is determined by dividing the total fixed costs by the variable-cost margin. Fractional quantities should be rounded up. Thus, there are two steps in the process of calculating the break-even point.

Step 1: Determine the variable cost margin per unit.

$$\frac{\text{Selling Price}}{\text{per Unit}} - \frac{\text{Variable Costs}}{\text{per Unit}} = \frac{\text{Variable-Cost Margin}}{\text{per Unit}}$$

Step 2: Calculate the break-even point in units.

$$\text{Total Fixed Costs} \div \text{Variable-Cost Margin} = \text{Break-even Point}$$

Example: The Omni Chemical Company produces a chemical called bromide that is used in swimming pools and hot tubs. The product sells to wholesalers or retailers for $8.40 for a 16-ounce container. Variable costs to produce this product are $5.50 per container. Total fixed costs are $340,000. How many 16-ounce containers (units) must be produced to reach the break-even point?

Step 1: Determine the variable-cost margin per unit.

$$\frac{\text{Selling Price}}{\text{per Unit}} - \frac{\text{Variable Costs}}{\text{per Unit}} = \frac{\text{Variable-Cost}}{\text{Margin per Unit}}$$

$$\$8.40 - \$5.50 = \$2.90$$

Step 2: Calculate the break-even point in units.

$$\frac{\text{Total}}{\text{Fixed Costs}} \div \frac{\text{Variable-Cost}}{\text{Margin}} = \frac{\text{Break-even}}{\text{Point}}$$

$$\$340,000 \div \$2.90 = 117,241 \text{ units}$$

This means that the Omni Chemical Company must sell 117,241 sixteen-ounce containers (units) of bromide to break even. If they sell less than this quantity, they will lose money; if they sell more, they will make a profit.

14 Learning Activity

Determine the break-even point for the following situations.

Total Fixed Costs	Selling Price per Unit	Variable Costs per Unit	Break-even Point in Units
$225,000	$4.50	$3.75	_____
$80,000	$10.00	$9.15	_____
$55,000	$7.50	$7.00	_____
$290,650	$15.50	$14.35	_____
$50,000	$4.50	$2.50	_____

Name _____ Date _____ Score _____

SECTION 3
USING MATH IN MARKETING

1. Explain why proper pricing is important to a businessperson.

   To earn an income from the efforts they make and the risks they take.

2. Define the following pricing terms as you understand them.

   a. Retail Price *The price at which merchandise is offered to the customer*

   b. Selling Price *The price at which merchandise is actually sold*

   c. Cost Price *The amount of merchandise paid by the business to a wholesaler or manufacturer*

   d. Initial Markup *The difference between the original retail price and the cost of merchandise*

   e. Maintained Markup *The difference between the selling price and the cost of merchandise*

3. Determine the retail price on each of the following items. Record your answers in the spaces provided.

Cost	Initial Markup	Retail Price
a. $22.60	$11.99	$ 34.59
b. $17.50	$8.00	$ 25.50
c. $0.89	$0.17	$ 1.06
d. $150.00	$75.00	$ 225.00

   e. The cost price of a video cassette recorder is $179.00. The VCR has an initial markup of $99.50. Determine the retail price.

   Retail Price $ 278.50

89

4. Determine the initial markup on each of the following items. Record your answers in the spaces provided.

	Retail Price	Cost	Initial Markup
a.	$22.50	$14.00	$_____
b.	$2.00	$1.15	$_____
c.	$8.65	$5.00	$_____
d.	$225.00	$150.00	$_____

e. The cost price of a suit is $89.65. The retail price for the suit is $159.00. Determine the initial markup.

Initial Markup $_____

5. Determine the cost of each of the following items. Record your answers in the spaces provided.

	Retail Price	Initial Markup	Cost
a.	$23.00	$9.20	$_____
b.	$1.06	$0.27	$_____
c.	$225.00	$75.00	$_____
d.	$99.95	$45.00	$_____

e. The retail price for an AM/FM cassette recorder is $29.95. The initial markup is $15.00. Determine the cost.

Cost $_____

6. Determine the initial markup as a percentage of cost for the following items. Record your answers in the spaces provided below. Round your answers to the nearest tenth of one percent.

	Cost	Initial Markup	Initial Markup as Percentage of Cost
a.	$7.20	$4.80	_____ %
b.	$175.00	$87.50	_____ %
c.	$0.78	$0.31	_____ %
d.	$1.65	$0.55	_____ %

e. The cost price of a motorcycle is $650.00. The initial markup is $312.00. Determine the initial markup percentage based on cost.

IM% (cost) _____ %

7. Determine the initial markup as a percentage of the retail price for the following items. Record your answers in the spaces provided. Round your answers to the nearest tenth of one percent.

Retail Price	Initial Markup	Initial Markup as Percentage of Retail
a. $10.00	$2.50	_____ %
b. $225.00	$75.00	_____ %
c. $1.10	$0.33	_____ %
d. $2.20	$0.55	_____ %

e. The retail price of a motorcycle is $900.00. The initial markup is $270.00. Determine the initial markup percentage based on retail.

IM% (retail) _____ %

8. For the items listed below, determine the initial markup and the retail price using the *cost method*. Record your answers in the spaces provided.

Item	Cost	Markup on Cost	Initial Markup	Retail Price
a. Gloves	$6.50	40%	$_____	$_____
b. Shirt	$9.00	50%	$_____	$_____
c. Shoes	$19.00	35%	$_____	$_____
d. Suit	$99.00	$66\frac{2}{3}$%	$_____	$_____

e. The cost price of a personal stereo cassette player is $35.00. The suggested initial markup is 40 percent. Determine the retail price using the cost method.

Retail Price (cost method) $_____

9. Find the retail prices for the items listed below, using the *retail method*. Record your answers in the spaces provided.

Item	Cost	Markup on Retail	Retail Price
a. Gloves	$6.50	40%	$_____
b. Shirt	$9.00	50%	$_____
c. Shoes	$19.00	35%	$_____
d. Suit	$99.00	$66\frac{2}{3}$%	$_____

e. The cost price of a compact disc player is $90.00. The suggested initial markup is 40 percent. Determine the retail price using the retail method.

Retail Price (retail method) $____120.____

10. For the items listed below, find the cost price the business could afford to pay.

Item	Retail Price	Markup on Retail	Cost
a. Golf clubs	$229.95	60%	$_____
b. Golf shoes	$19.50	46%	$_____
c. Golf balls	$1.79	58%	$_____
d. Tennis rackets	$45.00	35%	$_____
e. Can of tennis balls	$4.98	$66\frac{2}{3}$%	$_____

11. Using Table 3-1, determine the percentage markup on cost, the initial markup, and the retail price for each item listed below. Record your answers in the spaces provided.

Article	Cost	Markup on Retail	Markup on Cost	Initial Markup	Retail Price
a. Floor lamp	$47.95	$28\frac{1}{2}$%	____40____ %	$_____	$____67.13____
b. Swivel rocker	$133.00	$33\frac{1}{3}$%	____50____ %	$____166.50____	$____199.50____
c. Vertical blinds	$70.00	40%	____66.7____ %	$____116.69____	$____116.69____
d. End table	$62.00	50%	____100____ %	$____62.____	$____124____

Name _____

12. Determine the dollar markdown and the sale price on the following items. Record your answers in the spaces provided.

Item	Retail Price	Markdown	Dollar Markdown	Sale Price
a. Shirt	$16.00	25%	$_____ 4	$_____ 12.00
b. Shoes	$32.00	15%	$_____ 4.80	$_____ 27.20
c. Socks	$4.25	50%	$_____ 2.13	$_____ 2.12
d. Sport jacket	$90.00	$33\frac{1}{3}$%	$_____ 30	$_____ 60.00

13. Determine the dollar markdown, the sale price, and the percentage of maintained markup on the following items. Record your answers in the spaces provided.

Item	Cost	Retail Price	Markdown	Dollar Markdown	Sale Price	Maintained Markup
a. Compact disc	$15.00	$22.00	25%	$_____ 50	$_____ 16.50	_____ 90 %
b. Record	$2.55	$5.00	15%	$_____ .75	$_____ 4.25	_____ 40 %
c. Tape	$5.00	$9.95	20%	$_____	$_____ 7.96	_____ 37.4 %
d. Dual-cassette recorder	$65.00	$105.00	$33\frac{1}{3}$%	$_____ 35	$_____ 70.	_____ 7 %

14. Determine the price of one item, given the following units and total prices.

Item	Quantity	Total Price	Price of One Item (Unit)
a. Paper towels	3 rolls	$1.50	_____ ¢ per roll
b. Apples	1 dozen	$1.79	_____ 15 ¢ per apple
c. Donuts	12	$1.99	_____ ¢ per donut
d. Canned soup	24 cans	$7.20	_____ ¢ per can
e. Candy bars	4	$1.00	_____ 25 ¢ per candy bar

15. Find the price for the fractional quantities given below.

Number Desired	Price per Unit	Price for Fractional Quantity
a. $\frac{3}{4}$ yard cloth	$5.99/yard	$_____
b. $\frac{1}{2}$ pound hamburger	$1.89/pound	$_____
c. 3 cans of frozen orange juice	$2.79/six cans	$_____
d. $\frac{1}{3}$ pound of potatoes	$0.29/pound	$_____
e. $\frac{2}{3}$ dozen rolls	$1.00/dozen	$_____

16. Find the unit selling price for the following items.

Item and Price	Price/Unit
a. 10 oranges for $2.29	$_____ per dozen
b. 3 shirts for $12.99	$_____ per dozen
c. 36 ball-point pens for $10.55	$_____ per gross (144/gross)
d. 10-ounce package of raisins for 98¢	$_____ per pound
e. 50 sheets of bond paper for $1.79	$_____ per ream (500 sheets/ream)

17. Find the break-even point for the following items.

	Total Fixed Costs	Selling Price per Unit	Variable Costs per Unit	Break-even Point in Units
a.	$77,000	$14.00	$10.00	_____
b.	$15,000	$45.00	$42.00	_____
c.	$229,700	$40.50	$32.15	_____
d.	$32,400	$8.75	$7.95	_____
e.	$450,000	$30.00	$22.50	_____

SECTION 3
PROJECTS

3-1 PROJECT GOAL: To improve your understanding of pricing.

Step 1 From a catalog or newspaper ad, find the retail price of each of the following items. Given the markup percentage, determine the cost price for each item. Record your answers in the spaces provided below. Remember:

$$\text{Cost} = \text{RP}(100\% - \text{M}\%)$$

Product	Retail Price	Markup	Cost
a. Men's shirt	$_____	42%	$_____
b. Men's slacks	$_____	$33\frac{1}{3}\%$	$_____
c. Men's sport coat	$_____	50%	$_____
d. Women's bathing suit	$_____	60%	$_____
e. 12″ portable TV set (black & white)	$_____	30%	$_____
f. 35-mm camera	$_____	75%	$_____
g. Recliner chair	$_____	20%	$_____
h. Compact disc player	$_____	$66\frac{2}{3}\%$	$_____

Step 2 When you finish this project, compare your results with your classmates' results. Explain why you think cost prices vary.

3-2 PROJECT GOAL: To improve your understanding of how to calculate dollar markdown and percent of markdown.

Using a local newspaper, select five products advertised at sale prices. Record the following information in the spaces provided below: name of product, original retail price, special sale price, dollar markdown, and percent of markdown based on the retail price.

Product	Retail Price	Special Sale Price	Dollar Markdown	Percent Markdown
1. _____	$_____	$_____	$_____	_____%
2. _____	$_____	$_____	$_____	_____%
3. _____	$_____	$_____	$_____	_____%
4. _____	$_____	$_____	$_____	_____%
5. _____	$_____	$_____	$_____	_____%

SECTION 4
COMPLETING DAILY CALCULATIONS IN MARKETING

Many of the daily activities of a business selling merchandise or services involve math calculations. For instance, opening the cash register and verifying the accuracy of the change fund must be done every day. Both cash and charge sales transactions are handled during the day. Closing the cash register and proving the cash fund occurs at the end of every business day.

As you read this section, study the sample problems that are presented. By doing the problems at the end of this section correctly, you will show that you understand how to complete daily calculations in marketing.

After completing this section, you will be able to:

1. Verify the accuracy of the opening change fund.

2. Complete the calculations required for cash and charge sales, sales taxes, sales returns and exchanges, employee discounts, and merchandise discounts.

3. Make change accurately.

4. Prove the cash drawer at the end of the business day.

OPENING THE CASH REGISTER AND VERIFYING THE OPENING CHANGE FUND

At the start of each business day, a supply of change for the day must be put into the cash register drawer. This supply of change is called an *opening change fund*. The amount in this fund will depend on the type of merchandise or services sold and the amount of business expected during the day. Follow these steps when placing the opening change fund in the cash register drawer.

Step 1: Pick up the opening change fund from the appropriate person or location in your business. (In some businesses the change fund will be placed in the cash register drawer for you.) The change fund is the amount of money that the business makes available for each cash register at the beginning of the business day.

Step 2: Remove the cash drawer and place the change fund on a stiff piece of cardboard large enough to cover the bill compartment on the back half of the cash drawer as shown in Figure 4-1.

Figure 4-1
The Opening Change Fund

Step 3: There is a specific compartment in the cash drawer for each denomination of coins and currency, as shown in Figure 4-2. From left to right the front compartments are for half dollars, quarters, dimes, nickels, and pennies. Half dollars are not often used, but you may occasionally take some in during the day's business activities. Currency is placed in the cash drawer with the twenties behind the quarters, the tens behind the dimes, the fives behind the nickels, and the ones behind the pennies. Bills of $50 and $100, as well as checks, are placed underneath the removable cash drawer.

Figure 4-2
The Cash Drawer

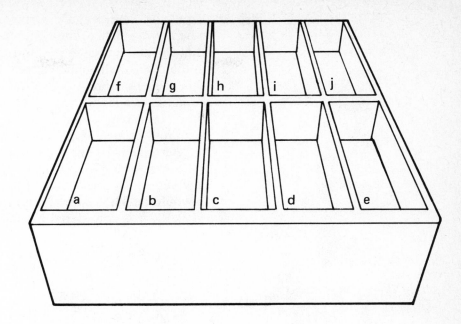

a. Half dollars   **f.** Remains empty
b. Quarters   **g.** $20 bills
c. Dimes   **h.** $10 bills
d. Nickels   **i.** $5 bills
e. Pennies   **j.** $1 bills

Step 4: Count the coins, one denomination at a time, and slide them into the appropriate compartments in the cash drawer. Next, count the currency. List both coins and currency as shown in Figure 4-3.

Figure 4-3
Listing Coins and Currency

Pennies	50
Nickels	40
Dimes	50
Quarters	24
Halves	10
$1.00	15
$5.00	10
$10.00	5
$20.00	3

Step 5: Total the change and currency that you have listed. Decide whether the change fund is even, over, or short. *Even* means that the amount of money in the change fund is equal to the amount originally planned for the cash drawer. *Over* indicates that there is more money, and *short* means that the change fund has less money than originally planned. If you find that the change fund is over or short, notify your manager or supervisor immediately. Figure 4-4 shows how the change fund total is determined. In this example, the originally planned change fund was $193.50. If the change fund count totaled $194.00, it would be 50¢ over. If the change fund count totaled $190.00, it would be $3.50 short. Since the change fund count totaled $193.50, it is considered even.

Figure 4-4
Totaling the Change Fund

Pennies	50	$ 0.50
Nickels	40	2.00
Dimes	50	5.00
Quarters	24	6.00
Halves	10	5.00
$1.00	15	15.00
$5.00	10	50.00
$10.00	5	50.00
$20.00	3	60.00

Total $193.50   (Actual Count of Change)

1
Learning Activity

Briefly list the five steps you would follow in opening the cash register and verifying the accuracy of the opening change fund.

Step 1:

Step 2:

Step 3:

continued

Step 4:

Step 5:

2
Learning Activity

In the illustration below, identify where the different denominations of coins and currency would be placed in the cash drawer.

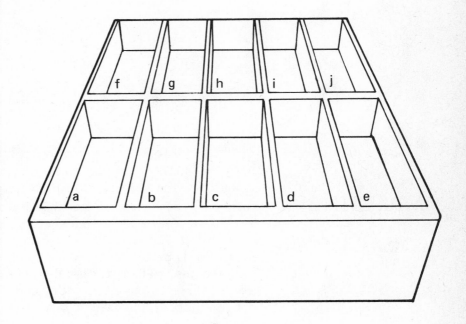

a. _____   f. _____

b. _____   g. _____

c. _____   h. _____

d. _____   i. _____

e. _____   j. _____

The Children's Department begins each day's activities with a $225.00 opening change fund. After the change fund was counted and placed in the cash drawer, the amounts were as follows:

Pennies	50	$_____
Nickels	25	$_____
Dimes	25	$_____
Quarters	40	$_____
Halves	5	$_____
Dollars	15	$_____
Fives	10	$_____
Tens	8	$_____
Twenties	3	$_____

Total $_____

The opening change fund was _____ even, _____ over, _____ short. Check one.

COMPLETING SALES TRANSACTIONS

Whenever a business sells merchandise or a service, a record of the transaction is always made. This record can be produced automatically by the cash register or manually by the salesperson writing a sales slip. These records become the "source documents"—the basis for operational records vital to successful business operations. Accurate sales records are very important to the profitability and success of a business.

The majority of businesses today use cash registers to maintain sales and inventory records. Information can be entered into the cash register manually by using the keyboard or automatically by using an electronic scanner (wand). An electronic scanner reads the information contained on the package of the merchandise or on the price ticket. Information entered into the cash register via either method is the same as the information written manually on a sales check.

Cash Sales Check

When a sales check is not written manually, the cash register receipt serves as the sales check. A cash register receipt is automatically issued when information about the sale is entered using the cash register keyboard. It is important that you understand the information shown on a printed sales check. Study the cash register sales check in Figure 4-5.

Illus. 4-1

The cash register produces a sales check automatically when the salesperson rings up merchandise.

Figure 4-5
Cash Register Sales Check

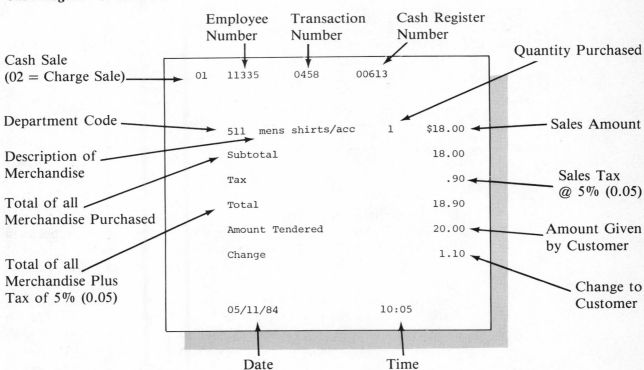

The information that is printed automatically by the cash register must be written out when a manually prepared sales check is used. Compare the information on the sales check in Figure 4-6 with the information printed by the cash register in Figure 4-5.

Figure 4-6
Manual Sales Check

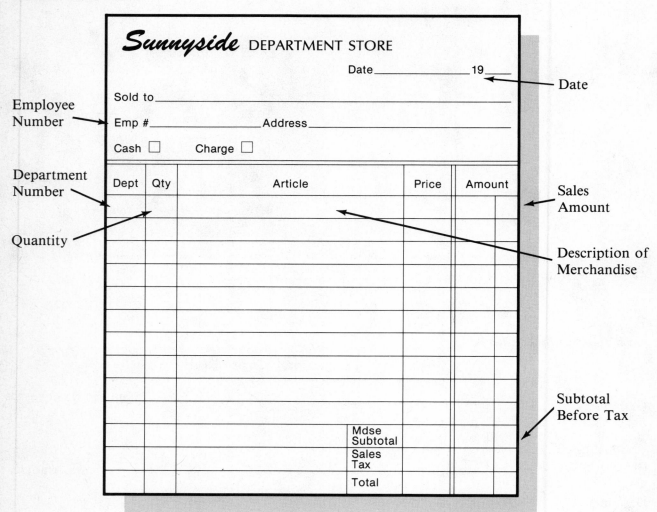

To prepare a sales check manually, the salesperson must be able to multiply and add correctly. Since many customers buy more than one item of merchandise, the salesperson must multiply the number of items (quantity) times the price per item. For example, if a customer bought two shirts at $15.95 each, the amount listed on the sales check would be $31.90. If the same customer bought three pairs of socks at $2.50 each, one pair of pants at $19.95, and a sweater at $25.00, the sales would be listed on the sales check as in Figure 4-7. The subtotal of the sales check is found by simply adding all of the amounts together.

Figure 4-7
Using Math on a
Manual Sales Check

Sunnyside DEPARTMENT STORE

Date_____ 19_____

Sold to_____

Emp #_____ Address_____

Cash ☐   Charge ☐

Dept	Qty	Article	Price	Amount
		Mdse Subtotal		
		Sales Tax		
		Total		

Illus. 4-2

Today, many cash registers in grocery stores display the items purchased and categorize the items for inventory in addition to totaling the customer's sales check.

Photo courtesy of NCR

Identify the various parts of the sales check below.

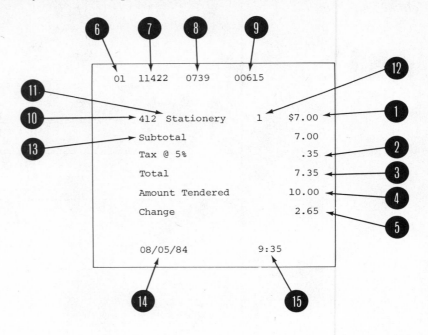

1. _____

2. _____

3. _____

4. _____

5. _____

6. _____

7. _____

8. _____

9. _____

10. _____

11. _____

12. _____

13. _____

14. _____

15. _____

5

Learning Activity

Using the information below, complete the following sales checks.

Sales Check A

Employee Number 157
Terms of Sale: Cash
Date: Today's date

Sales Made

Dept	Qty	Item	Price
16	2	Pair denim jeans	$22.99
25	1	Rib knit skirt	$20.88
15	3	T shirts	$11.88
18	1	Travel bag	$10.50

Sales Check B

Employee Number 263
Terms of Sale: Cash
Date: Today's date

Sales Made

Dept	Qty	Item	Price
33	1	Pair pinch-pleat draperies	$44.80
33	3	Pkg. drapery hooks	$2.79
33	4	Pair window blinds	$16.99
37	2	Bedspreads	$39.99

Sales Check A

Sunnyside DEPARTMENT STORE

Date_____ 19____

Sold to_____

Emp #_____ Address_____

Cash ☐   Charge ☐

Dept	Qty	Article	Price	Amount
		Mdse Subtotal		
		Sales Tax		
		Total		

continued

Sales Check B

```
┌─────────────────────────────────────────────────┐
│  𝓢𝓾𝓷𝓷𝔂𝓼𝓲𝓭𝓮  DEPARTMENT STORE                    │
│                          Date_____19____ │
│                                                    │
│  Sold to_____ │
│                                                    │
│  Emp #_____Address_____ │
│                                                    │
│  Cash ☐      Charge ☐                              │
│                                                    │
│  Dept │ Qty │      Article      │ Price │ Amount   │
│                                                    │
│                                                    │
│                                                    │
│                                                    │
│                                                    │
│                                                    │
│                                                    │
│                                                    │
│                                                    │
│                                                    │
│                                    Mdse            │
│                                    Subtotal        │
│                                    Sales           │
│                                    Tax             │
│                                    Total           │
└─────────────────────────────────────────────────┘
```

Calculating Sales Tax

Most states and some localities collect a tax on merchandise sold. This sales tax is expressed as a percentage, such as 3%, $3\frac{1}{2}$%, 4%, $4\frac{3}{4}$%, 5%, $5\frac{1}{4}$%, 6%, or $6\frac{3}{4}$%. The easiest way to figure the amount of sales tax is to multiply the sales tax rate times the sales amount. Before you multiply, you must convert (change) the percentage to a decimal fraction.

The percentages given above would be converted to the following decimal fractions.

Percentage	Decimal Fraction
3%	0.03
$3\frac{1}{2}$%	0.035
4%	0.04
$4\frac{3}{4}$%	0.0475
5%	0.05
$5\frac{1}{4}$%	0.0525
6%	0.06
$6\frac{3}{4}$%	0.0675

The amount of tax is determined by multiplying the sales tax decimal times the sales amount. The tax is then added to the amount of the sale. For example, if the sales tax rate is 5 percent and the amount of the purchase is $10.00, the sales tax would be determined as follows:

$5\% = 0.05$ ← Decimal Fraction

$\$10.00 \times 0.05 = \$0.50$

$\$10.00 + \$0.50 = \$10.50$ ← Amount of Sale Including Tax

6 Learning Activity

Using a 6.25 percent tax rate, determine the tax and total amount due for the following items. Round the tax to the nearest cent.

Item	Price	Tax	Total Amount
Paint brush	$2.79	$_____	$_____
Shirt	$10.00	$_____	$_____
Gloves	$6.50	$_____	$_____
Watch	$74.95	$_____	$_____
Aspirin	$0.87	$_____	$_____
Apple	$0.19	$_____	$_____
Snow tires	$155.29	$_____	$_____
Electric toaster	$17.75	$_____	$_____

Most states provide a sales tax schedule for determining the amount of sales tax. (See Table 4-1, page 111.) Table 4-1 is for a state that has a $4\frac{3}{4}\%$ sales tax. In using this tax schedule, you simply look for the amount of the sale. To the right of the sale amount, you will find the sales tax amount. For example, if the amount of the sale is $49.95, the sales tax would be $2.37. This sales tax amount is then added to the sales amount to determine the total purchase price.

7 Learning Activity

Use Table 4-1 to determine the tax and total amount due for the following items.

Item	Price	Tax	Total Amount
Cassette tape	$9.99	$_____	$_____
Portable AM/FM radio	$76.50	$_____	$_____
Package of beef jerky	$3.49	$_____	$_____
Electronic game cartridge	$24.00	$_____	$_____

continued

Item	Price	Tax	Total Amount
Paperback book	$3.95	$_____	$_____
Roll of masking tape	$0.69	$_____	$_____
Jeans	$26.00	$_____	$_____
Playing cards	$1.29	$_____	$_____

8
Learning Activity

Complete the sales check below for a cash sale using the information provided. Be sure to include the correct sales tax using Table 4-1. Your employee number is 176. This is a cash sale. Use today's date.

Dept.	Qty.	Item	Price
35	2	Tubes toothpaste	$1.19
35	3	Cans shaving cream	$1.09
35	1	Bottle after-shave	$1.89
35	2	Packages of razor blades	$2.59

Sunnyside DEPARTMENT STORE

Date_____ 19____

Sold to_____

Emp #_____ Address_____

Cash ☐   Charge ☐

Dept	Qty	Article	Price	Amount
		Mdse Subtotal		
		Sales Tax		
		Total		

Table 4-1
State Sales Tax Schedule $4\frac{3}{4}\%$

$ .01-$11.68	$11.69-$23.47	$23.48-$35.26	$35.27-$47.05	$47.06-$58.84	$58.85-$70.63	$70.64-$82.42	$82.43-$94.21
.01- .10- .00	11.69-11.89- .56	23.48-23.68-1.12	35.27-35.47-1.68	47.06-47.26-2.24	58.85-59.05-2.80	70.64-70.84-3.36	82.43-82.63-3.92
.11- .31- .01	11.90-12.10- .57	23.69-23.89-1.13	35.48-35.68-1.69	47.27-47.47-2.25	59.06-59.26-2.81	70.85-71.05-3.37	82.64-82.84-3.93
.32- .52- .02	12.11-12.31- .58	23.90-24.10-1.14	35.69-35.89-1.70	47.48-47.68-2.26	59.27-59.47-2.82	71.06-71.26-3.38	82.85-83.05-3.94
.53- .73- .03	12.32-12.52- .59	24.11-24.31-1.15	35.90-36.10-1.71	47.69-47.89-2.27	59.48-59.68-2.83	71.27-71.47-3.39	83.06-83.26-3.95
.74- .94- .04	12.53-12.73- .60	24.32-24.52-1.16	36.11-36.31-1.72	47.90-48.10-2.28	59.69-59.89-2.84	71.48-71.68-3.40	83.27-83.47-3.96
.95- 1.15- .05	12.74-12.94- .61	24.53-24.73-1.17	36.32-36.52-1.73	48.11-48.31-2.29	59.90-60.10-2.85	71.69-71.89-3.41	83.48-83.68-3.97
1.16- 1.36- .06	12.95-13.15- .62	24.74-24.94-1.18	36.53-36.73-1.74	48.32-48.52-2.30	60.11-60.31-2.86	71.90-72.10-3.42	83.69-83.89-3.98
1.37- 1.57- .07	13.16-13.36- .63	24.95-25.15-1.19	36.74-36.94-1.75	48.53-48.73-2.31	60.32-60.52-2.87	72.11-72.31-3.43	83.90-84.10-3.99
1.58- 1.78- .08	13.37-13.57- .64	25.16-25.36-1.20	36.95-37.15-1.76	48.74-48.94-2.32	60.53-60.73-2.88	72.32-72.52-3.44	84.11-84.31-4.00
1.79- 1.99- .09	13.58-13.78- .65	25.37-25.57-1.21	37.16-37.36-1.77	48.95-49.15-2.33	60.74-60.94-2.89	72.53-72.73-3.45	84.32-84.52-4.01
2.00- 2.21- .10	13.79-13.99- .66	25.58-25.78-1.22	37.37-37.57-1.78	49.16-49.36-2.34	60.95-61.15-2.90	72.74-72.94-3.46	84.53-84.73-4.02
2.22- 2.42- .11	14.00-14.21- .67	25.79-25.99-1.23	37.58-37.78-1.79	49.37-49.57-2.35	61.16-61.36-2.91	72.95-73.15-3.47	84.74-84.94-4.03
2.43- 2.63- .12	14.22-14.42- .68	26.00-26.21-1.24	37.79-37.99-1.80	49.58-49.78-2.36	61.37-61.57-2.92	73.16-73.36-3.48	84.95-85.15-4.04
2.64- 2.84- .13	14.43-14.63- .69	26.22-26.42-1.25	38.00-38.21-1.81	49.79-49.99-2.37	61.58-61.78-2.93	73.37-73.57-3.49	85.16-85.36-4.05
2.85- 3.05- .14	14.64-14.84- .70	26.43-26.63-1.26	38.22-38.42-1.82	50.00-50.21-2.38	61.79-61.99-2.94	73.58-73.78-3.50	85.37-85.57-4.06
3.06- 3.26- .15	14.85-15.05- .71	26.64-26.84-1.27	38.43-38.63-1.83	50.22-50.42-2.39	62.00-62.21-2.95	73.79-73.99-3.51	85.58-85.78-4.07
3.27- 3.47- .16	15.06-15.26- .72	26.85-27.05-1.28	38.64-38.84-1.84	50.43-50.63-2.40	62.22-62.42-2.96	74.00-74.21-3.52	85.79-85.99-4.08
3.48- 3.68- .17	15.27-15.47- .73	27.06-27.26-1.29	38.85-39.05-1.85	50.64-50.84-2.41	62.43-62.63-2.97	74.22-74.42-3.53	86.00-86.21-4.09
3.69- 3.89- .18	15.48-15.68- .74	27.27-27.47-1.30	39.06-39.26-1.86	50.85-51.05-2.42	62.64-62.84-2.98	74.43-74.63-3.54	86.22-86.42-4.10
3.90- 4.10- .19	15.69-15.89- .75	27.48-27.68-1.31	39.27-39.47-1.87	51.06-51.26-2.43	62.85-63.05-2.99	74.64-74.84-3.55	86.43-86.63-4.11
4.11- 4.31- .20	15.90-16.10- .76	27.69-27.89-1.32	39.48-39.68-1.88	51.27-51.47-2.44	63.06-63.26-3.00	74.85-75.05-3.56	86.64-86.84-4.12
4.32- 4.52- .21	16.11-16.31- .77	27.90-28.10-1.33	39.69-39.89-1.89	51.48-51.68-2.45	63.27-63.47-3.01	75.06-75.26-3.57	86.85-87.05-4.13
4.53- 4.73- .22	16.32-16.52- .78	28.11-28.31-1.34	39.90-40.10-1.90	51.69-51.89-2.46	63.48-63.68-3.02	75.27-75.47-3.58	87.06-87.26-4.14
4.74- 4.94- .23	16.53-16.73- .79	28.32-28.52-1.35	40.11-40.31-1.91	51.90-52.10-2.47	63.69-63.89-3.03	75.48-75.68-3.59	87.27-87.47-4.15
4.95- 5.15- .24	16.74-16.94- .80	28.53-28.73-1.36	40.32-40.52-1.92	52.11-52.31-2.48	63.90-64.10-3.04	75.69-75.89-3.60	87.48-87.68-4.16
5.16- 5.36- .25	16.95-17.15- .81	28.74-28.94-1.37	40.53-40.73-1.93	52.32-52.52-2.49	64.11-64.31-3.05	75.90-76.10-3.61	87.69-87.89-4.17
5.37- 5.57- .26	17.16-17.36- .82	28.95-29.15-1.38	40.74-40.94-1.94	52.53-52.73-2.50	64.32-64.52-3.06	76.11-76.31-3.62	87.90-88.10-4.18
5.58- 5.78- .27	17.37-17.57- .83	29.16-29.36-1.39	40.95-41.15-1.95	52.74-52.94-2.51	64.53-64.73-3.07	76.32-76.52-3.63	88.11-88.31-4.19
5.79- 5.99- .28	17.58-17.78- .84	29.37-29.57-1.40	41.16-41.36-1.96	52.95-53.15-2.52	64.74-64.94-3.08	76.53-76.73-3.64	88.32-88.52-4.20
6.00- 6.21- .29	17.79-17.99- .85	29.58-29.78-1.41	41.37-41.57-1.97	53.16-53.36-2.53	64.95-65.15-3.09	76.74-76.94-3.65	88.53-88.73-4.21
6.22- 6.42- .30	18.00-18.21- .86	29.79-29.99-1.42	41.58-41.78-1.98	53.37-53.57-2.54	65.16-65.36-3.10	76.95-77.15-3.66	88.74-88.94-4.22
6.43- 6.63- .31	18.22-18.42- .87	30.00-30.21-1.43	41.79-41.99-1.99	53.58-53.78-2.55	65.37-65.57-3.11	77.16-77.36-3.67	88.95-89.15-4.23
6.64- 6.84- .32	18.43-18.63- .88	30.22-30.42-1.44	42.00-42.21-2.00	53.79-53.99-2.56	65.58-65.78-3.12	77.37-77.57-3.68	89.16-89.36-4.24
6.85- 7.05- .33	18.64-18.84- .89	30.43-30.63-1.45	42.22-42.42-2.01	54.00-54.21-2.57	65.79-65.99-3.13	77.58-77.78-3.69	89.37-89.57-4.25
7.06- 7.26- .34	18.85-19.05- .90	30.64-30.84-1.46	42.43-42.63-2.02	54.22-54.42-2.58	66.00-66.21-3.14	77.79-77.99-3.70	89.58-89.78-4.26
7.27- 7.47- .35	19.06-19.26- .91	30.85-31.05-1.47	42.64-42.84-2.03	54.43-54.63-2.59	66.22-66.42-3.15	78.00-78.21-3.71	89.79-89.99-4.27
7.48- 7.68- .36	19.27-19.47- .92	31.06-31.26-1.48	42.85-43.05-2.04	54.64-54.84-2.60	66.43-66.63-3.16	78.22-78.42-3.72	90.00-90.21-4.28
7.69- 7.89- .37	19.48-19.68- .93	31.27-31.47-1.49	43.06-43.26-2.05	54.85-55.05-2.61	66.64-66.84-3.17	78.43-78.63-3.73	90.22-90.42-4.29
7.90- 8.10- .38	19.69-19.89- .94	31.48-31.68-1.50	43.27-43.47-2.06	55.06-55.26-2.62	66.85-67.05-3.18	78.64-78.84-3.74	90.43-90.63-4.30
8.11- 8.31- .39	19.90-20.10- .95	31.69-31.89-1.51	43.48-43.68-2.07	55.27-55.47-2.63	67.06-67.26-3.19	78.85-79.05-3.75	90.64-90.84-4.31
8.32- 8.52- .40	20.11-20.31- .96	31.90-32.10-1.52	43.69-43.89-2.08	55.48-55.68-2.64	67.27-67.47-3.20	79.06-79.26-3.76	90.85-91.05-4.32
8.53- 8.73- .41	20.32-20.52- .97	32.11-32.31-1.53	43.90-44.10-2.09	55.69-55.89-2.65	67.48-67.68-3.21	79.27-79.47-3.77	91.06-91.26-4.33
8.74- 8.94- .42	20.53-20.73- .98	32.32-32.52-1.54	44.11-44.31-2.10	55.90-56.10-2.66	67.69-67.89-3.22	79.48-79.68-3.78	91.27-91.47-4.34
8.95- 9.15- .43	20.74-20.94- .99	32.53-32.73-1.55	44.32-44.52-2.11	56.11-56.31-2.67	67.90-68.10-3.23	79.69-79.89-3.79	91.48-91.68-4.35
9.16- 9.36- .44	20.95-21.15-1.00	32.74-32.94-1.56	44.53-44.73-2.12	56.32-56.52-2.68	68.11-68.31-3.24	79.90-80.10-3.80	91.69-91.89-4.36
9.37- 9.57- .45	21.16-21.36-1.01	32.95-33.15-1.57	44.74-44.94-2.13	56.53-56.73-2.69	68.32-68.52-3.25	80.11-80.31-3.81	91.90-92.10-4.37
9.58- 9.78- .46	21.37-21.57-1.02	33.16-33.36-1.58	44.95-45.15-2.14	56.74-56.94-2.70	68.53-68.73-3.26	80.32-80.52-3.82	92.11-92.31-4.38
9.79- 9.99- .47	21.58-21.78-1.03	33.37-33.57-1.59	45.16-45.36-2.15	56.95-57.15-2.71	68.74-68.94-3.27	80.53-80.73-3.83	92.32-92.52-4.39
10.00-10.21- .48	21.79-21.99-1.04	33.58-33.78-1.60	45.37-45.57-2.16	57.16-57.36-2.72	68.95-69.15-3.28	80.74-80.94-3.84	92.53-92.73-4.40
10.22-10.42- .49	22.00-22.21-1.05	33.79-33.99-1.61	45.58-45.78-2.17	57.37-57.57-2.73	69.16-69.36-3.29	80.95-81.15-3.85	92.74-92.94-4.41
10.43-10.63- .50	22.22-22.42-1.06	34.00-34.21-1.62	45.79-45.99-2.18	57.58-57.78-2.74	69.37-69.57-3.30	81.16-81.36-3.86	92.95-93.15-4.42
10.64-10.84- .51	22.43-22.63-1.07	34.22-34.42-1.63	46.00-46.21-2.19	57.79-57.99-2.75	69.58-69.78-3.31	81.37-81.57-3.87	93.16-93.36-4.43
10.85-11.05- .52	22.64-22.84-1.08	34.43-34.63-1.64	46.22-46.42-2.20	58.00-58.21-2.76	69.79-69.99-3.32	81.58-81.78-3.88	93.37-93.57-4.44
11.06-11.26- .53	22.85-23.05-1.09	34.64-34.84-1.65	46.43-46.63-2.21	58.22-58.42-2.77	70.00-70.21-3.33	81.79-81.99-3.89	93.58-93.78-4.45
11.27-11.47- .54	23.06-23.26-1.10	34.85-35.05-1.66	46.64-46.84-2.22	58.43-58.63-2.78	70.22-70.42-3.34	82.00-82.21-3.90	93.79-93.99-4.46
11.48-11.68- .55	23.27-23.47-1.11	35.06-35.26-1.67	46.85-47.05-2.23	58.64-58.84-2.79	70.43-70.63-3.35	82.22-82.42-3.91	94.00-94.21-4.47

Charge Sales

When a customer makes a purchase using a credit card, a charge sales check (such as the one shown in Figure 4-8) is completed. One copy of the completed charge sales check is kept by the business as the record of the sale. Another copy becomes the customer's receipt for the purchase. Notice that the information contained on the charge sales check is basically the same as that on the cash register receipt and cash sales

Illus. 4-3

The information contained on the charge sales slip is basically the same as that on the cash register receipt and cash sales slip.

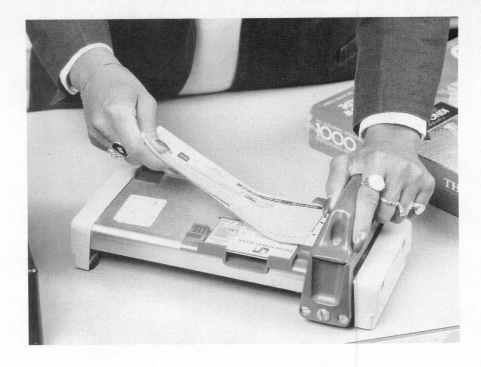

slip discussed earlier. The various parts of the charge sales check have been numbered and are explained immediately following Figure 4-8.

Figure 4-8
Charge Sales Check

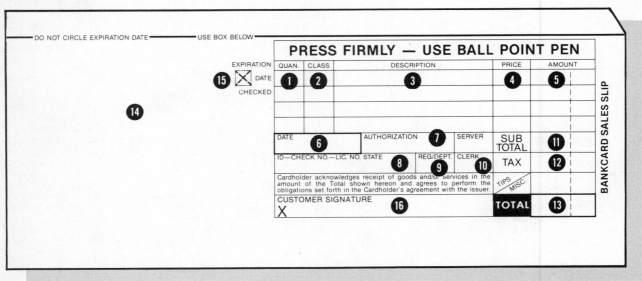

1. *Quan.*—Quantity purchased or number of items purchased by customer.

2. *Class*—Merchandise stock number.

3. *Description*—Brief one- or two-word description of merchandise purchased.

4. *Price*—Cost per item of merchandise.

5. *Amount*—Quantity multiplied times the price.

6. *Date*—Date of the sale.

7. *Authorization*—Usually required for sales of more than $50.00. This code (usually a series of numbers) is obtained by calling a toll-free telephone number of the company or bank issuing the credit card. More and more marketing businesses are using automatic computerized systems for the approval of all credit card sales. Credit cards contain a magnetic code or strip that contains all of the necessary customer information. When read through an automatic credit card approval machine, the sale is either approved or disapproved by a computer located at a central location. An authorization code will be shown in a small display window of the credit card approval machine.

8. *ID—Check No.—Lic. No. State*—Driver's license number or other customer identification number.

9. *Reg/Dept.*—The number assigned to the department or cash register.

10. *Clerk*—The initials of the salesperson recording the sale.

11. *Subtotal*—Total of purchases before sales tax.

12. *Tax*—Sales tax at appropriate rate.

13. *Total*—Subtotal plus tax.

14. *Credit Card Imprint*—Duplicates cardholder's name, account number, and card expiration date from face of credit card.

15. *Expiration Date Checked*—Reminder to salesperson to check credit card expiration date.

16. *Customer Signature*—Customer signs here after all other information is completed.

Illus. 4-4

Many businesses use automatic credit card approval machines.

Examine how the following sales information is entered on the charge sales check in Figure 4-9.

Date: January 14, 19--

Authorization: Not applicable because purchase is less than $50.00.

Customer Identification Number: 1053729

Sales Tax Rate: 5%

Sold By: Debbie Baker (DB)

Department Number: 55

Items Sold:

Quantity	Class	Description	Price
1	45	Pair shoes	$25.00
3	37	Pair socks	$3.50
1	45	Can shoe polish	$1.29

Figure 4-9
Entering Information on a
Charge Sales Check

Complete the following charge sales check using the information provided below.

9
Learning Activity

1. Dept. No. 41
2. Your initials
3. Customer Identification Number: 403716

continued

4. Date: Today's date

5. Authorization: 1-76-322

6. Sales Tax Rate: 5%

7. Items Sold:

Quantity	Class	Description	Price
1	371	Pair skis	$209.50
1	350	Ski sweater	$35.00
1	320	Pair ski boots	$59.95
3	321	Pair ski socks	$3.95

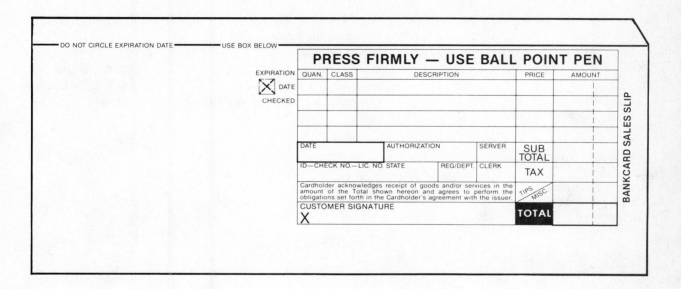

Accepting Checks

Customers frequently pay for merchandise or services with personal checks. Policies for accepting personal checks vary from one business to the next, but most follow general guidelines such as the following.

1. Personal checks are usually only accepted for the amount of the purchase.

2. A maximum limitation on the amount of the personal check that may be accepted without authorization may be established by the business owner or manager.

3. Personal checks should be filled out correctly and completely and made payable to the business. Checks made out to another person (multiple-endorsement or two-party checks) should not be accepted.

4. Stale-dated checks (checks bearing a date more than 30 days old) or post-dated checks (checks bearing a future date) should not be accepted.

5. Customers paying by personal check should be requested to provide two positive forms of identification. A driver's license with a picture and a major credit card are usually sufficient. Many customers will also have a bank check-guarantee card. This card means the bank guarantees checks up to $50.00 or $100.00.

6. Out-of-state checks will usually require the approval of management.

When customers pay for merchandise or services by using payroll checks, travelers checks, or government checks, you should follow the same procedures as for personal checks. In addition, new federal regulations have established specific areas on the back of checks to be used for endorsements. All endorsements (signatures) must appear in the area illustrated in Figure 4-10. Specifically, the endorsements must appear within *one and one-half inches* of the right end of the back of the check. (The right end of the back of the check is the left end of the front of the check.) When accepting payroll or government checks (such as social security checks), make sure that the payee's (customer's) signature appears in the area shown in Figure 4-10. If the signature falls below the $1\frac{1}{2}$ inches, the bank will not accept the check for deposit into the business's account.

Figure 4-10
New Requirements
Regarding Check
Endorsements

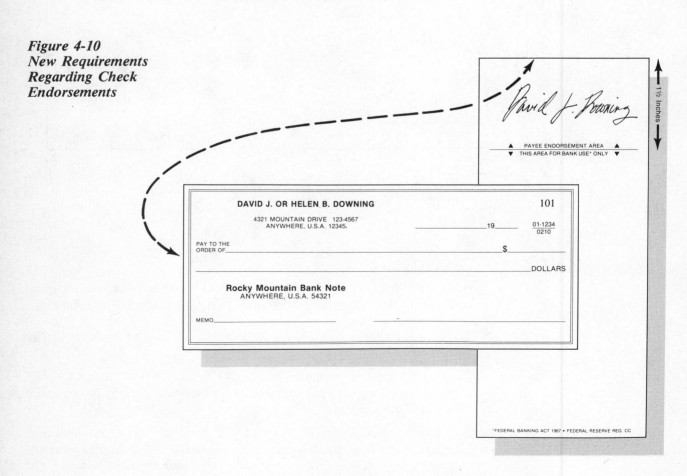

Policies regarding taking payroll and government checks will vary from one business to the next, because these checks usually result in cash back to the customer.

When a customer presents a personal check for payment of merchandise or services, the salesperson should follow the steps below.

Step 1: Make sure the check is filled out accurately. It should contain the correct date, the correct amount, and a complete signature. The customer's correct address and phone number should be preprinted on the face of the check.

Step 2: Politely ask the customer for two forms of identification or a check guarantee card.

Step 3: Record the required information on the front of the check along the top or bottom border. Prior to the Federal Banking Act of 1987, all of the essential identification information was recorded on the back of the check. This law limited the back of the check for endorsements, which must appear in the top $1\frac{1}{2}$ inches of the check. (See Figure 4-10.)

Step 4: Stamp or write "For Deposit Only" in the top $1\frac{1}{2}$ inches of the back of the check. Most businesses will have a deposit stamp.

Step 5: Follow the procedure/policy of the business regarding who is authorized to approve checks.

10 Learning Activity

Complete the information on the front of the check in the margin at the top of the check.

Driver's License No.: 275364457

State: Ohio

Credit Card No.: 6197654-76

Issued By: First National Bank

JENNIFER HODGES
4590 WALNUT AVENUE   555-2513
LOGAN, OHIO   57976-3299

866

April 11 19 90   97-7075/1211

PAY TO THE ORDER OF _The Card Shop_ $ 10 00

Ten _____ 00/100 DOLLARS

FIRST NATIONAL BANK
479 West Boulevard
Logan, Ohio 57976-3299

FOR CLASSROOM USE ONLY

MEMO _____   _Jennifer Hodges_

⑆ 121170758 ⑆ 0866 ⑈ 0150039113 ⑈

DELUXE CHECK PRINTERS - LH

11
Learning Activity

What five steps should be followed by the salesperson when accepting a check?

Step 1:

Step 2:

Step 3:

Step 4:

Step 5:

Sales Returns and Exchanges

Sometimes customers return merchandise for cash refund, for credit to their charge accounts, or in exchange for other merchandise. When merchandise is exchanged for other merchandise that is less expensive, the customer must be refunded the difference plus the tax charges on this difference. (Or, his or her charge account may be credited.) For example, if a customer returns a shirt that costs $10.00 and exchanges it for a shirt that costs $8.00, the difference due the customer would be $2.00 ($10.00 − $8.00 = $2.00). The tax on the difference of $2.00 at 5 percent would be 10¢ ($2.00 × 0.05 = 10¢) for a total refund of $2.10.

If, however, this transaction is reversed and the customer returns an $8.00 shirt in exchange for one that costs $10.00, the difference payable by the customer would be $2.00. The additional sales tax would be 10¢ for a total difference of $2.10 payable by the customer.

12
Learning Activity

For the following sales exchanges, calculate the amount of refund or amount payable by the customer. The sales tax rate is 5 percent.

1. Returned 1 gallon of paint that cost $12.95.
   Exchanged for 1 gallon of paint at $10.75.

   Dollar difference $_____. Tax on difference $_____.

   Total amount to be refunded to customer $_____.

continued

2. Returned 1 suit that cost $149.95.
Exchanged for 1 sport coat at $82.95.

Dollar difference $_____. Tax on difference $_____.

Total amount to be refunded to customer $_____.

3. Returned 1 electric knife that cost $22.50.
Exchanged for 1 electric roaster at $39.95.

Dollar difference $_____. Tax on difference $_____.

Total amount due by customer $_____.

4. Returned 1 nylon winter coat that cost $69.87.
Exchanged for leather coat at $84.97.

Dollar difference $_____. Tax on difference $_____.

Total amount due by customer $_____.

Cash Refund Slips

When cash is paid out to a customer for merchandise returned, a refund slip is usually completed. An example of a cash refund slip is shown in Figure 4-11. Most businesses will provide cash refunds to customers if they have a good reason for wanting to return the merchandise and if the merchandise is in its original condition and can be resold. The various parts of this form are numbered and explained following the sample form.

Figure 4-11
Cash Refund Slip

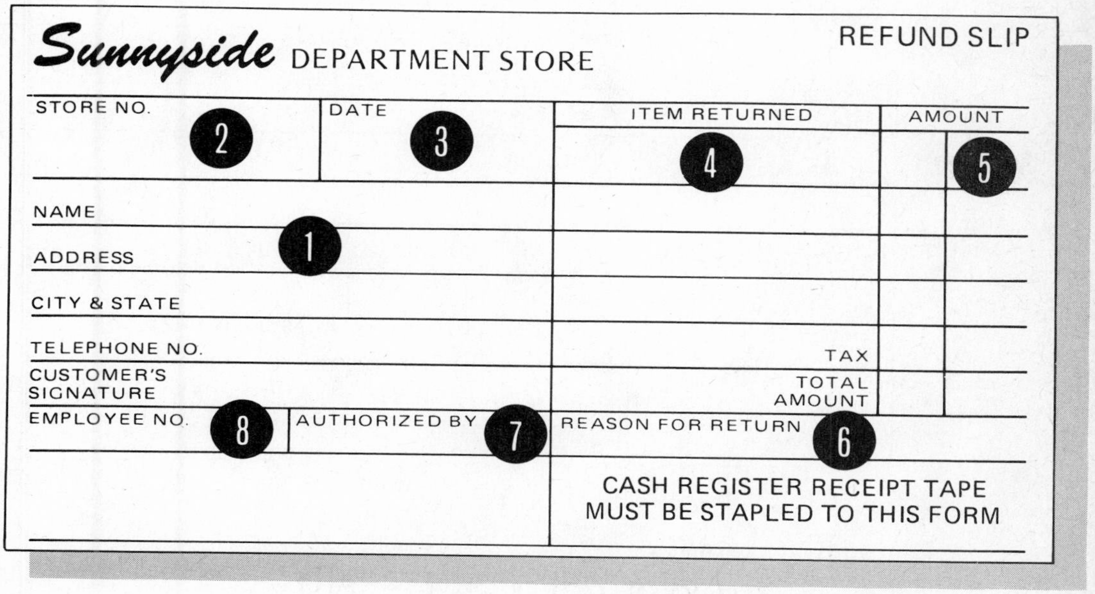

1. *Customer Information*—Information about the customer returning the merchandise, such as name, address, city and state, telephone number, and customer's signature.

2. *Store Number*—Number assigned to business or store.

3. *Date*—Date merchandise returned.

4. *Item Returned*—Description of item(s) returned.

5. *Amount*—Dollar amount of item(s) returned.

6. *Reason for Return*—Customer's explanation of why merchandise is being returned.

7. *Authorized By*—Signature of person in your business who has authority to approve cash refunds.

8. *Employee Number*—The number assigned to you as an employee.

13
Learning Activity

Using the information given, complete the cash refund forms.

Refund Slip A

1. Employee No. 188

2. Store No. 12

3. Customer Information:
   Name: Rose Andersen
   Address: 1501 State St.
   City & State: Clear Lake, IA
   Telephone: 555-2991

4. Date: Today's date

5. Item: 1 pair shoes @ $40.00

6. Tax Rate: 5%

7. Reason for Return:
   Wrong color

Sunnyside DEPARTMENT STORE			REFUND SLIP
STORE NO.	DATE	ITEM RETURNED	AMOUNT
NAME			
ADDRESS			
CITY & STATE			
TELEPHONE NO.		TAX	
CUSTOMER'S SIGNATURE		TOTAL AMOUNT	
EMPLOYEE NO.	AUTHORIZED BY	REASON FOR RETURN	
		CASH REGISTER RECEIPT TAPE MUST BE STAPLED TO THIS FORM	

continued

Refund Slip B

1. Employee No. 188
2. Store No. 12
3. Customer Information:
   Name: Sam Moore
   Address: 501 Sycamore
   City & State: Clear Lake, IA
   Telephone: 555-4469
4. Date: Today's date
5. Item: 1 golf bag @ $69.95
   1 golf glove @ $12.00
6. Tax Rate: $4\frac{1}{2}$%
7. Reason for Return:
   Duplicate gifts

Sunnyside DEPARTMENT STORE   REFUND SLIP

STORE NO.	DATE	ITEM RETURNED	AMOUNT

NAME

ADDRESS

CITY & STATE

TELEPHONE NO.   TAX

CUSTOMER'S SIGNATURE   TOTAL AMOUNT

EMPLOYEE NO.   AUTHORIZED BY   REASON FOR RETURN

CASH REGISTER RECEIPT TAPE
MUST BE STAPLED TO THIS FORM

Employee Discounts

Many businesses allow their employees a discount on merchandise they buy, as a type of fringe benefit. At the same time, this policy encourages employees to buy from the businesses where they work. The following example will help you understand how to calculate employee discounts.

Example: Swallow's Department Store allows all employees a 25 percent discount on purchases. A purchase made by an employee is $50.00. Determine the cost (amount of sale) to the employee.

Step 1: Change the percentage discount to the decimal 0.25.

Step 2: Multiply the decimal percentage times the amount of the purchase to find the amount of the discount. $0.25 \times \$50.00 = \$12.50$.

Step 3: Subtract the amount of the discount ($12.50) from the purchase price ($50.00) to determine the cost (the amount of the sale) to the employee. $50.00 − $12.50 = $37.50 cost to employee.

The employee would pay sales tax on the discounted amount.

For the following employee purchases, determine the amount of discount and the cost to the employee.

Employee Purchase	Discount	Amount of Discount	Cost to Employee
$83.99	20%	$_____	$_____
$11.49	10%	$_____	$_____
$21.50	15%	$_____	$_____
$112.00	33%	$_____	$_____
$65.00	50%	$_____	$_____

Merchandise Markdowns or Discounts

At certain times of the year, businesses will offer merchandise on a discounted basis to their customers. Discounts are given on merchandise or services for several different reasons. The business may be trying to attract new customers, or the business may be trying to reduce its inventory of merchandise. Merchandise discounts may be computed the same way as employee discounts or they may follow another procedure. Study the example below to understand this other procedure.

Example: Lakeland Sporting Goods is selling its downhill skis for 60 percent off during the month of April. A customer purchased a set of skis with an original retail price of $249.00. Determine the sale or discounted price to the customer.

Step 1: Subtract the 60 percent from 100 percent. Change the percentage to a decimal.

$$100\% - 60\% = 40\%$$
$$40\% = 0.40$$

Step 2: Multiply the resulting decimal (0.40) times the original retail price ($249.00).

$$0.40 \times \$249.00 = \$99.60$$

This result is the sale or discounted new price the customer pays.

Calculate the sale or discount price to the customer for the following.

Item	Original Retail Price	Discount	Sale Price
Ski gloves	$39.95	20%	$_____
Ski bibs	$100.00	50%	$_____
Skis	$329.00	33%	$_____
Ski poles	$24.50	60%	$_____
Ski parka	$149.50	25%	$_____

MAKING PROPER CHANGE

Making accurate change is one of the most important duties of a salesperson. Many businesses use cash registers that automatically calculate the change due after the amount of the sale and the amount received from the customer have been entered into the cash register. (Some registers even issue the correct amount of coins to the customer.) Other registers show only the amount of the sale. The salesperson must then calculate the change due the customer.

Illus. 4-5

One of the most important responsibilities of a salesperson is being sure customers receive the correct change.

Automatic Change Calculation

When the cash register automatically calculates the amount of change due the customer after a purchase, it is easy to count out the change. After the sale is rung up, the amount of change due appears in the display window of the register and on the customer's receipt. For example, if a customer buys a pair of pants for $12.97 + 50¢ sales tax, the total due from the customer would be $13.47. If the customer gives the sales person $20.00, change of $6.53 would be automatically displayed by the cash register. In this example, the salesperson would say to the customer: "That was $13.47 out of $20.00. Your change is $6.53. $5.00 and $1.00 is $6.00 and 53¢." Always use the largest denomination of currency and coins available.

16
Learning Activity

For the following sales, use the fewest number of coins and currency to make change. Count silently to yourself the change due.

Amount of Sale	Amount Received	Change	$0.01	$0.05	$0.10	$0.25	$1.00	$5.00	$10.00
$0.19	$0.50	$0.31							
$1.39	$5.00	$3.61							
$9.78	$20.00	$10.22							
$2.76	$10.00	$7.24							
$1.46	$1.50	$0.04							
$0.42	$5.00	$4.58							
$5.49	$10.00	$4.51							
$0.52	$1.00	$0.48							

Manual Change Calculation

Many businesses still use cash registers that do not automatically calculate change due the customer. To count change manually, it is not necessary to add or subtract; instead, merely count money. Start counting with the amount of the sale and stop counting with the amount the customer gave you. It's that simple! For example, if a customer purchased merchandise for $2.54 and gave you $5.00, you would start counting with $2.54. Say, "That was $2.54 out of $5.00, $2.54, $2.55, $2.65, $2.75, $3.00, $4.00, and $5.00." Notice in the above transaction that each dollar denomination was mentioned. This process will prevent slipping or missing a dollar when counting back change. Again, use the fewest possible number of coins and currency.

17
Learning Activity

Using the fewest possible number of coins and currency, show the amount of change returned for each of the following transactions. Count silently to yourself the change due.

Amount of Sale	Amount Received	Denomination						
		$0.01	$0.05	$0.10	$0.25	$1.00	$5.00	$10.00
$2.71	$5.00							
$0.28	$0.50							
$11.32	$15.00							
$5.15	$10.00							
$2.15	$2.50							
$9.73	$20.00							
$26.21	$50.00							
$0.69	$1.00							

Odd-Cent Change

Sometimes, if the purchase totals a few cents over an even amount, the customer may give you the odd change in addition to the money for which change must be made. For example, let's assume the amount of the sale is $17.52. The customer may give you a $20 bill and two pennies. The procedure to follow is to just cancel out the odd pennies when determining the amount of change to give the customer. Say, "That was $17.50 out of $20.00. I have subtracted the 2¢ from the 52¢, $17.50, $17.75, $18.00, $19.00, and $20.00."

18
Learning Activity

For the following odd-cent change situations, write out how you would call out the change to the customer.

Purchase Amount	Amount Given by Customer
$1.26	$2.01

Say:

continued

Purchase Amount	Amount Given by Customer
$9.27	$10.07

Say:

$2.13	$5.13

Say:

PROVING THE CASH DRAWER

As you learned at the beginning of this section, all cash registers start the business day with an opening change fund. As sales are made during the day, the amount of money in the cash register drawer increases. At the end of the day's business activities, the total amount of cash received (including checks) is printed automatically on the detailed audit strip. The *detailed audit strip* is a paper tape within the cash register that records all cash register activity. The total amount of cash in the drawer, plus any cash paid out, minus the opening change fund should equal the total amount printed on the detailed audit strip. The process is called *proving cash*.

To prove cash at the end of the day, follow these steps:

Step 1: Count the cash in the register drawer by denomination and write down the total amount for each denomination on a piece of paper. Then add the denomination totals. Checks used to pay for merchandise should be added into the total. See the following example:

50	Pennies	$ 0.50
30	Nickels	1.50
35	Dimes	3.50
40	Quarters	10.00
50	$1 Bills	50.00
15	$5 Bills	75.00
4	$10 Bills	40.00
2	$20 Bills	40.00
1	Check	8.00
	Total Cash in Drawer	$228.50

Step 2: Next, add the receipts for cash paid out during the day. (Note: Each time money is paid out of the register drawer, such as payment for a delivery of merchandise, a receipt is filled out and placed in the cash drawer.) Add the total amount paid out to the cash in the register drawer. This will be the *total cash* for the day including money taken in sales transactions and the opening change fund. For example, if the total receipts for cash paid out is $6.50 and the total amount of cash in the cash drawer is $228.50, *total cash* for the day would be $235.00 ($228.50 + $6.50 = $235.00).

Step 3: From the total obtained in Step 2, subtract the amount of the opening change fund. The remainder will be the total amount of *cash received* during the day. For example, at the end of the day the total amount of cash determined in Step 2 was $235.00. If the opening change fund was $35.00, this would mean that $200.00 was received in sales transactions during the day ($235.00 − $35.00 = $200.00).

Step 4: Compare the amount of cash received during the day with the amount shown on the detailed audit strip. If the two totals agree, the cash is proved. If the total amount of cash received is larger than the amount appearing on the detailed audit strip, the cash is over. If it is less, the cash is short. For example, if the amount shown on the detailed audit strip is $200.00 and the amount taken in during the day is $200.00 (Step 3), the cash is considered proved.

A daily balance form, similar to the one shown in Figure 4-12, is frequently used in proving cash for the day. The daily balance form in Figure 4-12 has been completed by using the procedures given in Steps 1-4.

Figure 4-12
Daily Balance Form

Number	Denomination	Amount	
		Date: _____	
Number	**Denomination**	**Amount**	
50	Pennies	$ 0	50
30	Nickels	1	50
35	Dimes	3	50
40	Quarters	10	00
50	$1.00 Bills	50	00
15	$5.00 Bills	75	00
4	$10.00 Bills	40	00
2	$20.00 Bills	40	00
1	Check	8	00
	Cash in Drawer	228	50
	Plus Cash Paid Out	6	50
	Total Cash	235	00
	Less Opening Change	35	00
	Cash Received	200	00
	Cash Received, Detailed Audit Strip	200	00
	✔ Proved ____Cash Over ____Cash Short	Amount of Cash Over or Short	

Complete the following daily balance form, filling in the blanks where necessary. On the bottom of the form, check whether the cash is proved, over, or short.

Daily Balance Form

Date: _____

Number	Denomination	Amount	
75	Pennies	$	
36	Nickels		
50	Dimes		
20	Quarters		
40	$1.00 Bills		
10	$5.00 Bills		
8	$10.00 Bills		
5	$20.00 Bills		
2	Checks	32	45
	Cash in Drawer		
	Plus Cash Paid Out	10	00
	Total Cash		
	Less Opening Change	90	00
	Cash Received		
	Cash Received, Detailed Audit Strip	237	25
	_____Proved _____Cash Over _____Cash Short	Amount of Cash Over or Short	$

SECTION 4
USING MATH IN MARKETING

1. The following denominations of coins and currency are in four opening change funds. Determine the totals of these opening change funds.

a.

Pennies	25	$_____
Nickels	30	$_____
Dimes	20	$_____
Quarters	15	$_____
$1.00	10	$_____
$5.00	5	$_____
$10.00	3	$_____
$20.00	—	$_____
	Total	$_____

b.

Pennies	50	$_____
Nickels	25	$_____
Dimes	45	$_____
Quarters	27	$_____
$1.00	10	$_____
$5.00	10	$_____
$10.00	5	$_____
$20.00	5	$_____
	Total	$_____

c.

Pennies	75	$_____
Nickels	45	$_____
Dimes	30	$_____
Quarters	30	$_____
$1.00	25	$_____
$5.00	10	$_____
$10.00	5	$_____
$20.00	5	$_____
	Total	$_____

d.

Pennies	100	$_____
Nickels	40	$_____
Dimes	50	$_____
Quarters	20	$_____
$1.00	20	$_____
$5.00	15	$_____
$10.00	5	$_____
$20.00	—	$_____
	Total	$_____

2. Compare the amounts given, which were supposed to be in the opening change fund, with the actual count of the opening change fund. Indicate how much each amount is over or short.

	Amount Supposed to be in the Opening Change Fund	Actual Change Count	Amount Over or Short
Department A	$45.00	$48.75	$_____
Department B	$125.00	$125.00	$_____
Department C	$100.00	$98.75	$_____
Department D	$80.00	$80.25	$_____
Department E	$175.00	$169.85	$_____

3. In your own words, explain the five steps you would follow in opening the cash register for the business day and verifying the accuracy of the opening change fund.

Step 1:

Step 2:

Step 3:

Step 4:

Step 5:

4. In the following illustration of the cash drawer, identify where the different denominations of coins and currency should be placed.

a. _____   **f.** _____

b. _____   **g.** _____

c. _____   **h.** _____

d. _____   **i.** _____

e. _____   **j.** _____

Name _____

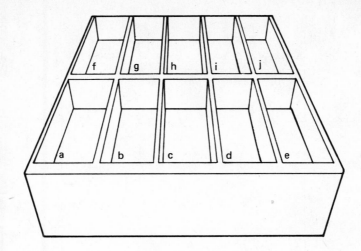

5. Using the sales tax schedule or tax rate for your state or area, determine the tax and the total amount payable by the customer for the following items. (If you do not have a tax schedule for your state or area, use a 5 percent tax rate.)

	Item	Price	Tax	Total Amount
a.	Variable speed drill	$59.50	$_____	$_____
b.	Metric socket wrench set	$35.82	$_____	$_____
c.	Bench vise	$27.95	$_____	$_____
d.	2-drawer file cabinet	$54.95	$_____	$_____
e.	Printing calculator	$34.90	$_____	$_____
f.	Electronic typewriter	$139.75	$_____	$_____
g.	Secretarial chair	$29.00	$_____	$_____
h.	Electric blanket	$19.29	$_____	$_____
i.	Mattress pad	$12.99	$_____	$_____
j.	Extra firm pillow	$10.00	$_____	$_____
k.	150″ traverse rod	$16.16	$_____	$_____
l.	Nylon rug (6′ × 9′)	$59.88	$_____	$_____
m.	Rattan chair	$79.55	$_____	$_____
n.	Tablecloth	$10.22	$_____	$_____
o.	One pair drapes	$31.99	$_____	$_____
p.	Clothes hamper	$22.00	$_____	$_____

6. Identify the various parts of the sales check shown below.

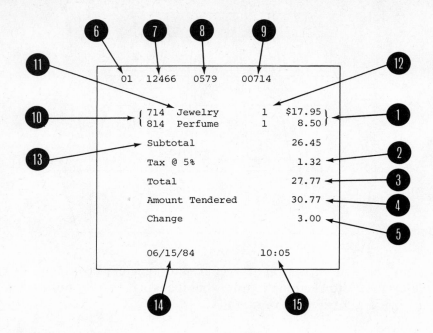

1. _____

2. _____

3. _____

4. _____

5. _____

6. _____

7. _____

8. _____

9. _____

10. _____

11. _____

12. _____

13. _____

14. _____

15. _____

Name _____

7. Given the following information, complete the four sales checks. Use a 6 percent tax rate.

Sales Check A

Employee Number 2014
Terms of Sale: Cash
Date: Today's date

Sales Made

Dept.	Qty.	Item	Price Each
52	1	Battery	$36.97
52	2	Fan belt	$6.95
55	4	Snow tires	$49.99
52	6	Qts. of oil	$1.19

Sunnyside DEPARTMENT STORE

Date_____19_____

Sold to_____

Emp #_____Address_____

Cash ☐   Charge ☐

Dept	Qty	Article	Price	Amount
		Mdse Subtotal		
		Sales Tax		
		Total		

Completing Daily Calculations in Marketing   133

Sales Check B

Employee Number 2056
Terms of Sale: Cash
Date: Today's date

Sales Made

Dept.	Qty.	Item	Price Each
26	1	Vacuum	$97.99
24	1	Set silverware	$44.97
24	6	Dish towels	$2.29
26	4	Pkgs. dust rags	$0.99

Sunnyside DEPARTMENT STORE

Date_____ 19_____

Sold to_____

Emp #_____ Address_____

Cash ☐   Charge ☐

Dept	Qty	Article	Price	Amount
		Mdse Subtotal		
		Sales Tax		
		Total		

Sales Check C

Employee Number 77
Terms of Sale: Cash
Date: Today's date

Sales Made

Dept.	Qty.	Item	Price Each
86	1	Microwave oven	$359.95
84	1	Set microwave cookware	$25.99
84	2	Microwave browning dishes	$14.95
86	1	Microwave oven cart	$34.95

Sunnyside DEPARTMENT STORE

Date _____ 19 ____

Sold to _____

Emp # _____ Address _____

Cash ☐   Charge ☐

Dept	Qty	Article	Price	Amount
		Mdse Subtotal		
		Sales Tax		
		Total		

Sales Check D

Employee Number 64
Terms of Sale: Cash
Date: Today's date

Sales Made

Dept.	Qty.	Item	Price Each
64	3	Pair cotton socks	$2.49
60	4	Knit shirts	$8.97
60	1	Pair sport boots	$34.99
60	1	Pair jeans	$19.25

Sunnyside DEPARTMENT STORE

Date_____ 19____

Sold to_____

Emp #_____ Address_____

Cash ☐   Charge ☐

Dept	Qty	Article	Price	Amount
		Mdse Subtotal		
		Sales Tax		
		Total		

8. Complete the charge sales checks using the information given.

Charge Sales Check A

1. Department No. 54
2. Your initials
3. Customer Identification Number: 4756-3824-59
4. Date: Today's date
5. Authorization: 1-33-674
6. Sales Tax Rate: 5%
7. Items Sold:

Quantity	Class	Description	Price
1	1254	Audio/video cabinet	$159.99
3	1253	Video tapes	$4.99
2	1252	Compact discs	$19.50

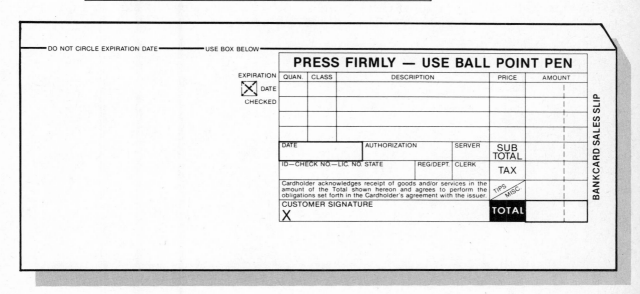

Charge Sales Check B

1. Department No. 22
2. Your initials
3. Customer Identification Number: SH135942
4. Date: Today's date
5. Authorization: NA
6. Sales Tax Rate: 5%
7. Items Sold:

Quantity	Class	Description	Price
2	321	Wool shirts	$24.99
3	323	Packages of handkerchiefs	$2.50
1	325	Pair gloves	$10.00

DO NOT CIRCLE EXPIRATION DATE — USE BOX BELOW —

PRESS FIRMLY — USE BALL POINT PEN

EXPIRATION [X] DATE CHECKED

QUAN.	CLASS	DESCRIPTION	PRICE	AMOUNT

DATE | AUTHORIZATION | SERVER | SUB TOTAL
ID—CHECK NO.—LIC. NO. STATE | REG/DEPT. | CLERK | TAX

Cardholder acknowledges receipt of goods and/or services in the amount of the Total shown hereon and agrees to perform the obligations set forth in the Cardholder's agreement with the issuer. | TIPS MISC.

CUSTOMER SIGNATURE
X

TOTAL

BANKCARD SALES SLIP

9. When presented with a personal check from a customer, what steps should you follow?

Step 1:

Step 2:

Step 3:

Step 4:

Step 5:

10. Customers returned the following items and exchanged them for merchandise costing less. Calculate the cost difference, the tax on the difference using the $4\frac{3}{4}$ percent tax schedule shown on page 111, and the total due each customer.

	Original Price	New Price	Cost Difference	Tax on Difference	Total Refunded to Customer
a.	$27.99	$24.99	$_____	$_____	$_____
b.	$9.00	$6.95	$_____	$_____	$_____
c.	$3.99	$2.29	$_____	$_____	$_____
d.	$59.50	$39.75	$_____	$_____	$_____
e.	$149.95	$79.95	$_____	$_____	$_____

11. Customers returned the following items and exchanged them for merchandise costing more. Calculate the cost difference, the tax on the difference using a $4\frac{1}{2}$ percent tax rate, and the total payable by each customer.

	Original Price	New Price	Cost Difference	Tax on Difference	Total Payable by Customer
a.	$12.99	$17.88	$_____	$_____	$_____
b.	$113.50	$217.19	$_____	$_____	$_____
c.	$3.79	$5.95	$_____	$_____	$_____
d.	$16.88	$18.99	$_____	$_____	$_____
e.	$39.95	$59.95	$_____	$_____	$_____

12. Calculate the amount of the employee discount and the cost to the employee for the following purchases.

	Retail Price	Discount	Amount of Discount	Cost to Employee
a.	$79.49	33%	$_____	$_____
b.	$35.50	40%	$_____	$_____
c.	$9.99	20%	$_____	$_____
d.	$5.47	25%	$_____	$_____
e.	$179.95	5%	$_____	$_____

13. Complete the following cash refund slip using the information provided.

1. Employee No. 213

2. Store No. 18

3. Customer Information:
   Name: Douglas Skanky
   Address: 1235 N 1500 E
   City & State: Salt Lake City, UT
   Telephone: 555-9410

4. Date: Today's date

5. Item: 1 compact disc player $240.00

6. Tax Rate: 5%

7. Reason for Return: lacks clear tone

Sunnyside DEPARTMENT STORE

REFUND SLIP

STORE NO.	DATE	ITEM RETURNED	AMOUNT
NAME			
ADDRESS			
CITY & STATE			
TELEPHONE NO.		TAX	
CUSTOMER'S SIGNATURE		TOTAL AMOUNT	
EMPLOYEE NO.	AUTHORIZED BY	REASON FOR RETURN	

CASH REGISTER RECEIPT TAPE
MUST BE STAPLED TO THIS FORM

14. Calculate the sale or discount price to the customer for the following.

Item	Original Retail Price	Discount	Sale Price
a. Audio tape	$3.99	15%	$_____
b. Tape head cleaner	$5.79	20%	$_____
c. Dual-cassette boom box	$99.95	$33\frac{1}{3}$%	$_____
d. Record album	$12.95	10%	$_____

15. Use the correct number of coins and currency to complete the following transactions. Count out the change silently to yourself.

	Amount of Sale	Amount Received	Change	$0.01	$0.05	$0.10	$0.25	$1.00	$5.00	$10.00	$20.00
a.	$1.56	$2.06									
b.	$79.95	$100.00									
c.	$0.39	$1.00									
d.	$9.50	$20.00									
e.	$49.67	$100.00									
f.	$6.76	$10.00									
g.	$21.00	$25.00									

16. For each sales transaction, write down how you would count out the change to the customer.

Transaction 1: Customer purchased basketball for $12.83. Gave salesperson $20.00.

Transaction 2: Customer purchased portable color TV set for $79.25. Gave salesperson $100.00.

Transaction 3: Customer purchased candy bar for 21¢. Gave salesperson $1.00.

Transaction 4: Customer purchased blouse for $21.17. Gave salesperson $25.00.

Transaction 5: Customer purchased electric drill bits for $5.27. Gave salesperson $10.27.

Transaction 6: Customer purchased 2 lb of nails of $1.31. Gave salesperson $2.01.

17. Complete the following daily balance form. On the bottom of the form, check whether the cash is proved, over, or short.

	Daily Balance Form		
	Date: _____		

Number	Denomination	Amount	
50	Pennies	$	
27	Nickels		
76	Dimes		
33	Quarters		
22	$1.00 Bills		
12	$5.00 Bills		
7	$10.00 Bills		
4	$20.00 Bills		
3	Checks	116	50
	Cash in Drawer		
	Plus Cash Paid Out	15	00
	Total Cash		
	Less Opening Change	100	00
	Cash Received		
	Cash Received, Detailed Audit Strip	256	20
	____Proved ____Cash Over ____Cash Short — Amount of Cash Over or Short	$	

SECTION 4
PROJECTS

4-1 PROJECT GOAL: To improve your skill in counting back change to customers.

Using a cash register or a simulated cash drawer, *role-play* (act out) counting back change to one of your fellow classmates. (Note: You may create your own money or your teacher may provide you with a money substitute for this project.)

	Purchase	Amount Received from Customer
a.	$11.95	$20.00
b.	$2.31	$3.01
c.	$2.75	$5.00
d.	$19.31	$50.00
e.	$22.50	$30.00
f.	$0.79	$1.09
g.	$79.33	$100.00
h.	$6.57	$10.57
i.	$3.22	$5.25
j.	$22.67	$25.00

4-2 PROJECT GOAL: To complete sales checks accurately.

Step 1 Complete the sales checks that follow, using today's date, your employee number of 572, and the tax schedule from your local community. The customer paid cash. All of the other information required to complete these sales checks will be found on the merchandise price tags given for each sale.

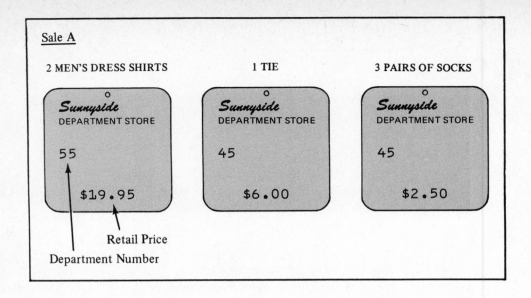

Sale A

2 MEN'S DRESS SHIRTS

Sunnyside
DEPARTMENT STORE

55

$19.95

Retail Price

Department Number

1 TIE

Sunnyside
DEPARTMENT STORE

45

$6.00

3 PAIRS OF SOCKS

Sunnyside
DEPARTMENT STORE

45

$2.50

Sale A

Sunnyside DEPARTMENT STORE					
Date_____ 19____					
Sold to_____					
Emp #_____Address_____					
Cash ☐ Charge ☐					

Dept	Qty	Article	Price	Amount	
			Mdse Subtotal		
			Sales Tax		
			Total		

Sale B

4 YARDS COTTON CLOTH	2½ YARDS OF RAYON	5 YARDS OF LACE TRIM
Sunnyside DEPARTMENT STORE	*Sunnyside* DEPARTMENT STORE	*Sunnyside* DEPARTMENT STORE
23	23	23
$1.69/YARD	$5.98/YARD	$.29/YARD

Sale B

Sunnyside DEPARTMENT STORE

Date _____ 19____

Sold to _____

Emp # _____ Address _____

Cash ☐   Charge ☐

Dept	Qty	Article	Price	Amount
		Mdse Subtotal		
		Sales Tax		
		Total		

Sale C

1 PAIR WOMEN'S DENIM JEANS

○
Sunnyside
DEPARTMENT STORE

18

$25.00

1 TURTLENECK SWEATER

○
Sunnyside
DEPARTMENT STORE

18

$32.50

Sale C

Sunnyside DEPARTMENT STORE

Date_____19___

Sold to_____

Emp #_____Address_____

Cash ☐   Charge ☐

Dept	Qty	Article	Price	Amount
		Mdse Subtotal		
		Sales Tax		
		Total		

Sale D

1 RACQUETBALL RACKET	2 CANS OF RACQUETBALLS	1 PAIR TENNIS SHOES
Sunnyside DEPARTMENT STORE	*Sunnyside* DEPARTMENT STORE	*Sunnyside* DEPARTMENT STORE
63	63	22
$29.95	$2.59	$18.50

Sale D

Sunnyside DEPARTMENT STORE

Date _____ 19 ____

Sold to _____

Emp # _____ Address _____

Cash ☐   Charge ☐

Dept	Qty	Article	Price	Amount
		Mdse Subtotal		
		Sales Tax		
		Total		

Step 2 **a.** Check your completed sales checks to make sure the information is complete.

b. Have another classmate check the accuracy of these four sales checks.

SECTION 5
UNDERSTANDING INVENTORY PROCEDURES

Keeping proper inventory records is critical to the success of a business. Any business that sells merchandise for a profit must always have merchandise available to sell. But too much merchandise waiting to be sold can be just as bad as not having enough to sell. Proper inventory procedures can help to maintain the correct amount of merchandise on hand at all times.

In this section you will learn about the different aspects of taking inventory. You will also learn how selected inventory information is used by a business. Study the terminology, ideas, and sample problems presented. Then complete the problems at the end of the section.

After completing this section, you will be able to:

1. Explain what a physical inventory is and how it is taken.

2. Identify the procedure followed in taking a physical inventory.

3. Explain perpetual inventory (book inventory) and how it is calculated.

4. Compare perpetual to physical inventory.

5. Convert retail value of ending inventory to cost value.

6. Calculate stock turnover rate.

7. Calculate open to buy.

149

PHYSICAL INVENTORY

At least once a year every business takes a physical inventory of merchandise on hand. During a physical inventory each unsold item is counted and recorded on a form called an *inventory sheet*. The major purpose of the physical inventory is to obtain an exact count of all merchandise on hand.

Taking a physical inventory is usually easier when two people work together. One person, the *caller*, counts the items and calls out the essential information. The other person, the *recorder*, records the information on an inventory sheet.

Inventory Sheets

Special inventory sheets are prepared in advance of inventory time. These sheets have spaces for recording the merchandise category number, description and item number, quantity, unit, price, season code, and total retail value. Although inventory sheets vary from one type of business to another, the one in Figure 5-1 contains all the information needed to complete an accurate inventory.

Figure 5-1
Inventory Sheet

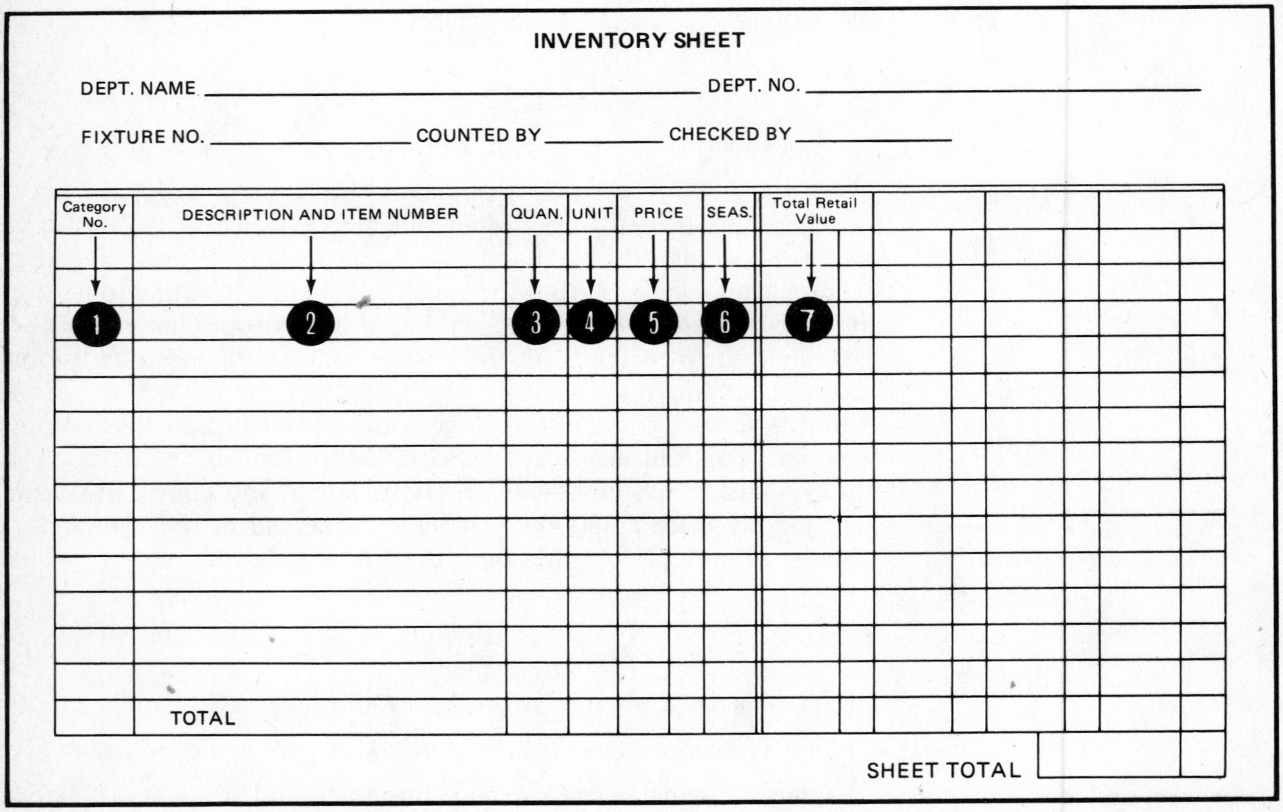

1. *Category Number*—Number code that corresponds to major classification of merchandise.

2. *Description and Item Number*—Brief word or words describing the type of merchandise and the number assigned to that item of merchandise.

3. *Quantity*—Total number of units or items of merchandise counted.

4. *Unit*—The quantity in which merchandise is sold. Example: ea = each, pr = pair, doz = dozen, pkg = package, bx = box, rl = roll.

5. *Price*—Retail price of each unit.

6. *Season*—Special code number indicating the age of merchandise or when it was purchased. A code might read 9-1, which indicates the merchandise was purchased during the ninth month (September), first day.

7. *Total Retail Value*—The product of the total quantity times the price.

Source of Information

The information written on the inventory sheet comes from the price tickets attached to the merchandise on the sales floor or in the stockroom. Usually merchandise that has just been received but not yet priced is excluded from the physical inventory. Figure 5-2 shows a typical price ticket.

Figure 5-2
Price Ticket

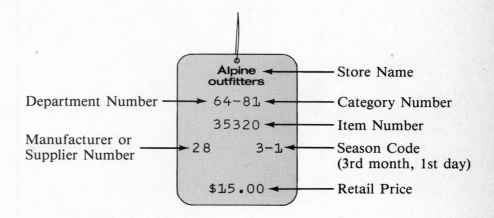

1 Learning Activity

Identify the information on the price ticket below.

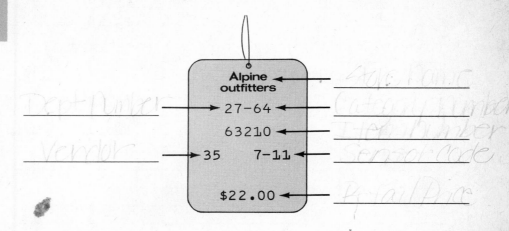

The information contained on price tickets must be transferred by the inventory recorder to the inventory sheet. If you were transferring the information from the following price tickets to an inventory sheet, you would record it as in Figure 5-3.

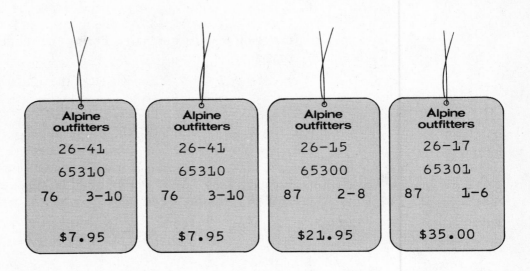

Figure 5-3
Recording Information
on an Inventory Sheet

INVENTORY SHEET

DEPT. NAME ___SPORTSWEAR___ DEPT. NO. ___26___

FIXTURE NO. ___27___ COUNTED BY ___ML___ CHECKED BY ___MP___

Category No.	DESCRIPTION AND ITEM NUMBER		QUAN.	UNIT	PRICE		SEAS.	Total Retail Value					
41	SHIRT	65310	2	EA	7	95	3-10	15	90				
15	SWEATER	65300	1	EA	21	95	2-8	21	95				
17	SWEATER	65301	1	EA	35	00	1-6	35	00				
	TOTAL												

SHEET TOTAL

2 Learning Activity

Record the information contained on these price tickets on the inventory sheet provided below.

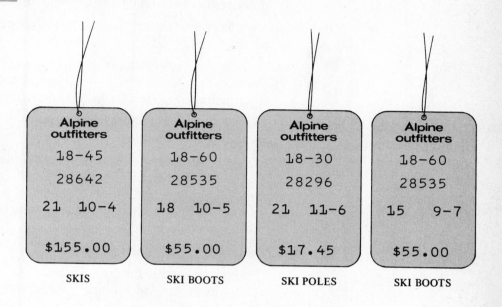

Alpine outfitters	Alpine outfitters	Alpine outfitters	Alpine outfitters
18-45	18-60	18-30	18-60
28642	28535	28296	28535
21 10-4	18 10-5	21 11-6	15 9-7
$155.00	$55.00	$17.45	$55.00
SKIS	SKI BOOTS	SKI POLES	SKI BOOTS

INVENTORY SHEET

DEPT. NAME SKI EQUIPMENT   DEPT. NO. 18

FIXTURE NO. 14   COUNTED BY SH   CHECKED BY WK

Category No.	DESCRIPTION AND ITEM NUMBER	QUAN.	UNIT	PRICE	SEAS.	Total Retail Value				
L	SKIS	1	EA	155	10-4	155 —				
10	SKI BOOTS 28535	1	EA	55	10-5	55 —				
30	SKI POLES 28296	1	EA	17 45	11-6	17 45				
10	SKI BOOTS 28535	1	EA	55	9-7	55 —				
	TOTAL									

SHEET TOTAL

Procedure to Follow in Taking a Physical Inventory

The physical inventory must be accurate and complete. To make sure it is, there are a number of rules to follow when taking a physical inventory.

1. Merchandise should be arranged by shelf or section, or in whatever manner the merchandise is to be recorded on the inventory sheet.

2. Do not erase. Rather, cross out with a pen or pencil to make corrections.

3. Do not use ditto marks (") when the same merchandise is listed on the next line. Use a wavy line to indicate the item is the same as the item just above. Do this in the description column only.

4. Do not leave spaces blank for quantity, unit, price, or season when recording merchandise.

5. Write carefully and clearly (printing is permitted) because someone else must read what you write. (Be especially careful as you write 1 and 7, 5 and 8, and 4 and 9. These numbers can be confused for one another.) Accurately write dollars in the dollar column and cents in the cents column.

6. Do not leave any lines blank.

7. Count merchandise on shelves left to right, top shelf first, then down. Leave the completed inventory sheet on the shelf in clear sight when finished.

8. The listing of description and item number, prices, season letters, and other information should be copied from the price tag—never from the stock book or other records.

Illus. 5-1

To take a physical inventory, start by counting the merchandise on the shelves left to right, top shelf first, then down.

9. Quantities of an item should be listed per item with the price entered per item. For example, it would be incorrect to list shirts at three for $20.00. Instead, the price should be listed at $6.66\frac{2}{3}$ for each shirt.

3
Learning Activity

Identify five of the nine things that should be done when completing a physical inventory.

1.

2.

3.

4.

5.

Calculating Inventory Extensions

Inventory extensions are completed after all of the merchandise has been counted and the necessary information recorded. An *extension* is the product of the quantity shown times the retail price. The total retail value of an inventory is the sum of all extensions. Study the extensions made on the inventory sheet in Figure 5-4 to better understand how to calculate extensions.

Figure 5-4
Calculating Inventory Extensions

INVENTORY SHEET

DEPT. NAME ___SHOES___ DEPT. NO. ___27___

FIXTURE NO. ___33___ COUNTED BY ___MM___ CHECKED BY ___BL___

Category No.	DESCRIPTION AND ITEM NUMBER		QUAN.	UNIT	PRICE		SEAS.	Total Retail Value						
3	MEN'S SHOES	15125	37	PR	21	95	2-10	812	15					
5	MEN'S SOCKS	10645	105	PR	2	50	3-7	262	50					
4	RUBBER BOOTS	15210	26	PR	9	95	1-5	258	70					
1	SHOELACES	10300	39	PR		75	3-9	29	25					
	TOTAL							1,362	60					

SHEET TOTAL 1,362 | 60

---

4 Learning Activity

Calculate the extensions on the following inventory sheet.

INVENTORY SHEET

DEPT. NAME ___PAINT___ DEPT. NO. ___25___

FIXTURE NO. ___15___ COUNTED BY ___GC___ CHECKED BY ___ML___

Category No.	DESCRIPTION AND ITEM NUMBER		QUAN.	UNIT	PRICE		SEAS.	Total Retail Value						
2	4" LATEX PAINT BRUSHES	436	24	EA	2	95	1-12							
4	PAINT THINNER	415	45	PT	1	39	3-2							
18	PAINT ROLLERS	318	16	EA	5	95	1-14							
16	LATEX ENAMEL PAINT	527	144	GA	10	50	8-17							
5	CAULKING COMPOUND	432	15	EA	1	79	6-12							
7	3" ROLL MASKING TAPE	430	75	EA	1	09	1-2							
8	PAINT REMOVER	419	18	PT	2	49	3-4							
12	LACQUER THINNER	420	12	GA	3	49	2-8							
	TOTAL													

SHEET TOTAL 1035 | 85

Inventory Sheet Requiring Limited Information

A very simple inventory sheet is used for fast-selling merchandise such as drug and grocery items. This type of sheet is used when no specific information is needed on each item of merchandise. When this type of inventory sheet is used, only the count of the number of items at each retail price is recorded. The person taking the inventory counts the items on a particular shelf or in a particular area and records the information under each price column provided. Figure 5-5 illustrates how a simple inventory sheet is filled out.

Figure 5-5
Simple Inventory Sheet

INVENTORY SHEET																						
Sheet No.: _____						Price Range From **50¢** to **59½¢**													Extension Total			
Date: _____																			Price	Quantity	Ext.	
50	50½	51	51½	52	52½	53	53½	54	54½	55	55½	56	56½	57	57½	58	58½	59	59½	50	44	$22.00
17	3			21			22	20	2		5		7	3		18	12		14	50½	38	19.19
15			10			14	2	4		10		8	7		9	14			12	51		
12	7		15			18		6		4		6				3			16	51½		
	18		8			19		7								5			8	52	68	35.36
	6		14			17		8								8			10	52½		
	4							12								10			14	53		
								14											8	53½	90	48.15
																			26	54	22	11.88
																			4	54½	53	28.89
																				55		
																				55½	19	10.55
																				56		
																				56½	21	11.87
																				57	10	5.70
																				57½		
																				58	27	15.66
																				58½	52	30.42
																				59		
																				59½	112	66.64
44	38			68			90	22	53		19		21	10		27	52		112	TOTAL	556	$306.31

Record the following information on the inventory sheet provided.

Quantity	Price	Quantity	Price	Quantity	Price
18	$20\frac{1}{2}$¢	27	24¢	7	$21\frac{1}{2}$¢
9	$21\frac{1}{2}$¢	15	$22\frac{1}{2}$¢	15	26¢
16	$22\frac{1}{2}$¢	6	$29\frac{1}{2}$¢	3	$29\frac{1}{2}$¢
6	24¢	6	$25\frac{1}{2}$¢	8	23¢
24	25¢	12	$26\frac{1}{2}$¢	16	26¢
3	$25\frac{1}{2}$¢	9	27¢	5	$23\frac{1}{2}$¢
5	26¢	3	28¢	25	20¢
13	27¢	12	$28\frac{1}{2}$¢	3	$20\frac{1}{2}$¢
8	$27\frac{1}{2}$¢	5	29¢	14	26¢
9	$24\frac{1}{2}$¢	4	26¢	6	$29\frac{1}{2}$¢

INVENTORY SHEET

Sheet No.: _____   Price Range From 20 ¢ to 29½ ¢

Date: _____

Extension Total

20	20½	21	21½	22	22½	23	23½	24	24½	25	25½	26	26½	27	27½	28	28½	29	29½	Price	Quantity	Ext.
																				20		
																				20½		
																				21		
																				21½		
																				22		
																				22½		
																				23		
																				23½		
																				24		
																				24½		
																				25		
																				25½		
																				26		
																				26½		
																				27		
																				27½		
																				28		
																				28½		
																				29		
																				29½		
																				TOTAL		

PERPETUAL INVENTORY

Most businesses maintain a continuous record of merchandise (stock) purchased and sold. Such a record is called a *perpetual inventory* (also known as *book inventory*). It can be computed at regular intervals (weekly, monthly, or even on a daily basis). Computerized electronic cash registers make maintaining a perpetual inventory much easier. Inventory information is entered through the cash register when merchandise is purchased. When an item is sold, it is automatically taken out of inventory, thus permitting a perpetual inventory.

If the perpetual inventory is accurately maintained, the business does not need to wait until a physical inventory is taken to find out what merchandise is in stock. With the aid of a perpetual inventory, the business can keep an ample supply of merchandise in stock to meet customer demand and, at the same time, keep its investment in stock as low as possible. The businessperson can also estimate profits from week to week or month to month using information taken from perpetual inventory records.

The perpetual inventory can be maintained by using the dollar value of merchandise or an actual count of units of merchandise in stock. With either method, the perpetual inventory is determined by adding purchases for the time period involved to the beginning inventory and then subtracting total sales from this figure. For example, if a business had a beginning physical inventory of $6,000, purchases during a six-month period of $41,000, and sales of $40,000, the perpetual inventory would be $7,000. This method can be used at any time, so the value or quantity of stock on hand can be known perpetually, or constantly.

Beginning Physical Inventory	$ 6,000
Purchases	+ 41,000
Total Merchandise Available for Sale	$47,000
Total Sales	− 40,000
Perpetual Inventory	$ 7,000

Illus. 5-2

In addition to reading prices, optical scanners record merchandise information for perpetual inventory.

6
Learning Activity

The Leather Shop had a beginning inventory of $19,000, purchases of $35,000, and sales of $38,000. Determine the perpetual inventory.

Beginning Physical Inventory	$_____
Purchases	$_____
Total Merchandise Available for Sale	$_____
Total Sales	$_____
Perpetual Inventory	$_____

Comparing Perpetual to Physical Inventory

When the semiannual or annual physical inventory is taken, the results are compared to the perpetual inventory to see if the results are equal. If both results are the same, the physical inventory is referred to as *even*. If the amount shown by the physical inventory is less than the perpetual inventory, the physical inventory is *short*. If the amount shown by the physical inventory is more than the perpetual inventory, the physical inventory is *over*.

Examples:	Physical Inventory	Perpetual Inventory	Even/Short/Over
	$27,500	$27,500	Even
	$27,500	$26,500	$1,000 Over
	$27,500	$28,500	$1,000 Short

7
Learning Activity

Compare the perpetual inventories to the physical inventories to determine if they are even, short, or over. If the physical inventory is over or short, show the amount. If the two inventories are even, put a check mark in the "Even" column.

Physical Inventory	Perpetual Inventory	Over	Short	Even
$37,500	$38,500	$_____	$_____	____
$105,700	$106,750	$_____	$_____	____
$76,900	$76,900	$_____	$_____	____
$235,000	$233,500	$_____	$_____	____
$29,800	$31,200	$_____	$_____	____

CONVERTING RETAIL VALUE OF ENDING INVENTORY TO COST VALUE

The ending physical inventory is taken using the retail value of the merchandise and must be converted to cost value in order to determine the cost of merchandise sold.

The retail method of pricing merchandise, as you learned earlier, is the most widely used method. To convert inventory (priced by the retail method) from retail value to cost value, multiply the average markup percentage on all purchases times the retail value of the inventory. The answer obtained from this calculation is then subtracted from the retail value of the inventory. The result is the cost value of the ending inventory. For example, if the value of the ending inventory at retail is $20,000 and the average markup on all merchandise is 40 percent, the ending inventory at cost would be $12,000. This figure is arrived at as follows:

Step 1:	$20,000	Ending Inventory at Retail
	× 0.40	Markup % as Decimal
	$8,000.00	Dollar Markup

Step 2:	$20,000	Ending Inventory at Retail
	− 8,000	Dollar Markup
	$12,000	Ending Inventory at Cost

8
Learning Activity

The ending physical inventory at retail for the Aquarium Shop is $18,000. The average markup on retail is $33\frac{1}{3}$ percent. Determine the ending inventory at cost.

$ _____

STOCK TURNOVER

With an adequate inventory system, the businessperson will know what merchandise is in stock. Inventory information can also help the businessperson to decide what new merchandise to purchase. The inventory system by itself, however, does not show how successful the business is. One way to estimate the success of a business is to calculate the stock turnover rate. The *stock turnover rate* is defined as the number of times during a given period that the inventory on hand has been completely sold and replaced. The stock turnover rate is usually measured on an annual basis but can also be calculated on a daily, weekly, monthly, or seasonal basis. Stock turnover can be calculated in terms of units, dollars, or both.

One way to estimate the success of a business is to calculate the stock turnover rate.

Unit Stock Turnover

Stock turnover in units is determined by dividing the total number of units sold by the average number of units in stock. First, you find the average number of units in stock (the average inventory) using the following formula:

$$\text{Average Inventory (Units)} = \frac{\begin{array}{c}\text{Sum of Beginning Inventories (Units)}\\ + \text{ Ending Inventory (Units) for a}\\ \text{Given Time Period}\end{array}}{\text{Number of Inventories}}$$

Suppose that an inventory is taken on the first day of each month for one year, and an ending inventory is taken on the last day of the last month. The sum of the 12 beginning inventories is 355 units and the ending inventory is 35 units. The number of inventories would be the 12 monthly beginning inventories plus the 1 ending inventory, for a total of 13. Substituting this information into the above formula will result in an average inventory of 30 units:

$$\text{Average Inventory (Units)} = \frac{355 + 35}{12 + 1}$$

$$\text{Average Inventory (Units)} = \frac{390}{13} = 30$$

The unit stock turnover rate can then be easily determined using the following formula:

$$\text{Stock Turnover Rate (Units)} = \frac{\text{Number of Units Sold}}{\text{Average Inventory}}$$

For example, if the recliner chair department of a furniture store had an average inventory of 30 recliner chairs and sold 120 per year, the annual stock turnover rate in units would be 4:

$$\text{Stock Turnover Rate (Units)} = \frac{\text{Number of Units Sold}}{\text{Average Inventory}} = \frac{120}{30} = 4$$

This means that the furniture store completely sold its inventory of recliner chairs four times during the year. The more times the stock of recliners is turned over, the greater the chance the business has to increase its profits from the sales of recliner chairs. (Note that both the average inventory and the unit stock turnover rate should be rounded to the nearest whole number.)

9
Learning Activity

Determine the average retail inventory and the unit stock turnover rate from the following information.

Sales: 500 pairs of shoes
Sum of 12 Monthly Beginning Inventories: 470
Ending Inventory: 30

Average Retail Inventory (Units)   _____

Unit Stock Turnover Rate   _____

Dollar Stock Turnover

Dollar stock turnover is calculated exactly the same way as unit stock turnover. Just substitute money amounts for unit amounts, using the following formula:

$$\text{Stock Turnover Rate (Dollars)} = \frac{\text{Net Sales (Dollars)}}{\text{Average Inventory (Dollars)}}$$

The first step in determining dollar stock turnover is to determine the average dollar inventory. The formula for calculating this figure is the same as that previously shown for average inventory in units except that dollars are used:

$$\text{Average Inventory (Dollars)} = \frac{\text{Sum of Beginning Inventories (Dollars)} + \text{Ending Inventory (Dollars) for a Given Time Period}}{\text{Number of Inventories}}$$

For example, if the sum of 12 monthly beginning inventories is $23,600, and the ending inventory is $2,400, the total value of the inventories for the year would be $26,000. This figure, $26,000, divided by the 13 inventories would result in an average monthly inventory of $2,000:

$$\text{Average Monthly Inventory (Dollars)} = \frac{\$23,600 + \$2,400}{13}$$

$$\text{Average Monthly Inventory (Dollars)} = \frac{\$26,000}{13} = \$2,000$$

If total sales for the year are $15,000, the stock turnover rate is found by dividing the annual sales by the average monthly inventory:

$$\text{Stock Turnover Rate} = \frac{\text{Annual Sales}}{\text{Average Monthly Inventory}}$$

$$\text{Stock Turnover Rate} = \frac{\$15,000}{\$2,000} = 7.5$$

10
Learning Activity

Determine the average monthly inventory and the dollar stock turnover rate using the following information.

Annual Sales: $127,000
Sum of 12 Monthly Beginning Inventories: $300,000
Ending Inventory: $28,000

Average Monthly Inventory (Dollars) $ _25230.77_

Dollar Stock Turnover Rate _5.03_

OPEN TO BUY

Information from an accurate inventory is also useful to a business in determining how much money is available for the purchase of new merchandise. This amount is known as *open to buy* (OTB). Generally, open to buy is figured on a monthly basis. To determine open to buy, a business must know the following:

1. *Estimated Sales for the Month*—The retail value of merchandise expected to be sold during the month.

2. *Estimated Stock at End of Month (EOM Inventory)*—The amount of merchandise remaining at the end of the month.

3. *Estimated Monthly Markdowns*—The expected reduction of the retail value of the inventory because of markdowns on certain merchandise.

4. *Beginning Inventory (BOM Inventory)*—The amount of inventory at the beginning of the month.

5. *Merchandise on Order*—The amount of merchandise on order for the month.

These five amounts are needed for the following open to buy formula:

$$OTB = \text{Estimated Sales} + \text{EOM Stock} + \text{Markdowns} - \text{BOM Stock} - \text{Merchandise on Order}$$

For example, if a business estimates sales of $12,000 for a month, estimates EOM stock of $22,000, estimates markdowns of $750, estimates BOM stock of $17,000, and has already ordered $5,000 worth of merchandise for the month, the businessperson would proceed as follows to calculate open to buy:

Estimated Sales	$12,000
Estimated EOM Stock	22,000
Estimated Markdowns	+ 750
	$34,750
BOM Stock	− 17,000
	$17,750
Merchandise on Order	− 5,000
OTB	$12,750

This business would have $12,750 available for the purchase of new merchandise.

Learning Activity

A business had estimated sales for April of $65,000, estimated EOM stock of $45,000, estimated markdowns of $1,200, and estimated BOM stock of $30,000. Orders for $9,000 have already been placed. Determine the open to buy figure for April.

$ _72,200_

SECTION 5
USING MATH IN MARKETING

1. Explain in your own words what the following parts of an inventory sheet mean.

    a. Category Number

    b. Description and Item Number

    c. Quantity

    d. Unit

    e. Price

    f. Season

    g. Total Retail Value

2. Identify the information on the following price ticket:

    1. _____

    2. _____

    3. _____

    4. _____

    5. _____

    6. _____

    7. _____

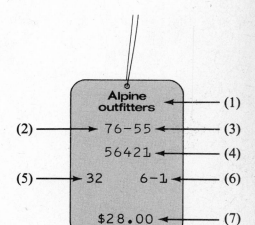

167

3. Enter the following information on the inventory sheet and calculate the extensions. Be sure to enter the totals at the bottom.

Category Number	Description	Item Number	Quantity	Unit	Season
55	Ladies' blouses	76542	28	$17.95	3-5
31	Ladies' pants	76300	14	$69.50	1-6
24	Ladies' sweaters	76400	6	$21.00	3-4
45	Ladies' dresses	76255	12	$40.00	3-4
25	Ladies' dresses	76258	15	$69.95	3-7

INVENTORY SHEET

DEPT. NAME _LADIES' WEAR_   DEPT. NO. _43_

FIXTURE NO. _11_   COUNTED BY _MQ_   CHECKED BY _DK_

Category No.	DESCRIPTION AND ITEM NUMBER	QUAN.	UNIT	PRICE	SEAS.	Total Retail Value					
	TOTAL										

SHEET TOTAL

4. Identify five of the nine procedures you should follow in taking a physical inventory.

Name _____

5. Calculate the extensions on the following inventory sheet.

INVENTORY SHEET

DEPT. NAME ___STATIONERY___ DEPT. NO. ___21___

FIXTURE NO. ___17___ COUNTED BY ___QK___ CHECKED BY ___WS___

1

Category No.	DESCRIPTION AND ITEM NUMBER	QUAN.	UNIT	PRICE	SEAS.	Total Retail Value				
65	MISC. CHRISTMAS CARDS 1865	17	BX	2 98	7-1					
49	GIFT WRAP ROLL 1860	38	RL	1 29	5-3					
18	ELECTRIC STAPLER 1340	12	EA	19 95	3-4					
76	5x7 WRITING TABLET 1250	27	EA	2 79	3-4					
55	CONSTRUCTION PAPER 1362	13	PKG	1 59	6-5					
12	ANNUAL CALENDARS 1518	24	EA	3 50	11-8					
18	MAGIC MARKERS 1230	69	EA	79	3-24					
16	MISC. PENCILS 1200	149	EA	39	3-24					
22	PAPER CLIPS 1500	49	BX	69	3-4					
	TOTAL									

SHEET

Understanding Inven

Sec

6. Enter the following merchandise on the simple inventory sheet provided. Complete each extension in the total section.

Quantity	Price	Quantity	Price	Quantity	Price	Quantity	Price
18	40¢	9	$45\frac{1}{2}$¢	3	$49\frac{1}{2}$¢	7	49¢
6	$47\frac{1}{2}$¢	3	43¢	8	$43\frac{1}{2}$¢	18	44¢
2	47¢	9	45¢	3	43¢	17	43¢
10	40¢	18	46¢	17	$41\frac{1}{2}$¢	13	46¢
3	$40\frac{1}{2}$¢	8	48¢	12	$43\frac{1}{2}$¢	23	$45\frac{1}{2}$¢
5	41¢	5	45¢	19	45¢	8	42¢
8	$47\frac{1}{2}$¢	7	41¢	6	43¢	12	45¢
7	$49\frac{1}{2}$¢	11	47¢	2	$49\frac{1}{2}$¢	12	$47\frac{1}{2}$¢
7	46¢	6	40¢	8	40¢	7	48¢
17	49¢	12	$46\frac{1}{2}$¢	16	$41\frac{1}{2}$¢	7	43¢

INVENTORY SHEET

Sheet No.: _____ Price Range From _40¢_ to _49½¢_

Date: _____

40	40½	41	41½	42	42½	43	43½	44	44½	45	45½	46	46½	47	47½	48	48½	49	49½	Price	Quantity	Ext.
																				40		
																				40½		
																				41		
																				41½		
																				42		
																				42½		
																				43		
																				43½		
																				44		
																				44½		
																				45		
																				45½		
																				46		
																				46½		
																				47		
																				47½		
																				48		
																				48½		
																				49		
																				49½		
																				TOTAL		

Name _____

7. The Real McCoy Dress Shop had a beginning physical inventory of $9,500, purchases of $37,000, and sales of $35,900 as of August 25. What amount should the perpetual inventory show on that date?

$_____

8. The Bicycle Shop had a beginning physical inventory of $10,000, purchases of $14,500, and sales of $11,500. Determine the perpetual inventory.

$_____

9. Determine the six-month perpetual inventory of a men's store from the following information. The July 1 beginning physical inventory was $4,750.

Month	Purchases	Sales
July	$3,000	$2,100
August	$2,600	$1,500
September	$5,500	$3,200
October	$6,200	$4,800
November	$4,100	$4,675
December	$1,150	$5,600

Perpetual Inventory on December 31 $_____

10. The perpetual inventory for a business is $128,500 and the ending physical inventory is $130,700. Compare the two inventories to determine if the business is even, short, or over in the physical inventory. If the inventories match, put a check mark in the blank next to "Even." If the physical inventory is over or short, show the amount.

Even   _____

Short $_____

Over $_____

11. If the ending physical inventory is $42,500 and the perpetual inventory shows $43,000, is the physical inventory even, short, or over the perpetual inventory? If it is even, put a check mark in the blank next to "Even." If it is over or short, show the amount.

Even _____

Short $_____

Over $_____

12. The ending physical inventory at retail for Smith's Grocery Store is $115,000. The average markup on retail is 16 percent. Determine the ending inventory at cost.

$_____

13. The ending physical inventory at retail for the Card Shop is $11,500. The average markup on retail is 40 percent. Determine the ending physical inventory at cost.

$_____

14. Using the following information for the Appliance Department at the Sunnyside Department Store, determine the average inventory and the annual stock turnover rate.

Unit Sales: 30 Refrigerators
Sum of 12 Monthly Beginning Inventories: 56 Refrigerators
Ending Inventory: 9 Refrigerators

Average Inventory (Units) _____

Stock Turnover Rate (Units) _____

15. Sunnyside Department Store sold 60 leather coats during the month of November. The average inventory of leather coats maintained in stock was 120. **(a)** Determine the stock turnover rate for the month of November. **(b)** Estimate the rate for the year.

a. _____

b. _____

16. The Valdez Hardware Store had annual sales of $175,250 and an average inventory of $60,000. What is the annual stock turnover rate for this business?

_____

17. The T-Shirt Factory had annual sales of $73,600 and an average inventory of $40,100. What is the annual stock turnover rate for this business?

_____

18. Using the following information for the Sporting Goods Department of Sunnyside Department Store, calculate the average inventory and the annual stock turnover rate.

Net Sales: $21,500
Sum of 12 Monthly Beginning Inventories: $67,925
Ending Inventory: $6,500

Average Inventory (Dollars) $_____

Stock Turnover Rate _____

19. The estimated sales for the Aquarium Shop are $5,500, estimated EOM stock is $3,850, estimated markdowns are $150, estimated BOM stock is $6,200, and merchandise on order for the month is $1,500. Determine the open to buy.

$ _____

20. Given the following information, determine the open to buy for each.

	Estimated Sales	Estimated EOM Stock	Estimated Markdowns	Estimated BOM Stock	Merchandise on Order	Open to Buy
a.	$20,000	$10,000	$800	$9,000	$5,800	$ _____
b.	$30,800	$39,500	$1,200	$36,000	$24,000	$ _____
c.	$38,200	$23,500	$550	$26,500	none	$ _____

SECTION 5
PROJECTS

5-1 PROJECT GOAL: To improve your understanding of inventory procedures.

Step 1 Individually or with a small group of your classmates study the inventory procedures used by two local businesses. Find out the following:

a. How physical inventory counts are made.

b. When and how frequently they are taken.

c. What information is contained on the price tags.

Step 2 Collect, if possible, sample inventory sheets or price tickets used by these businesses. Share your findings with your classmates.

5-2 PROJECT GOAL: To understand stock turnover rate and ways of increasing this figure.

Step 1 Visit three of the four different types of businesses identified below. Ask the manager to give you the estimated annual stock turnover rate for the business.

Type of Business	Estimated Stock Turnover Rate
Department Store	_____
Grocery Store	_____
Speciality Store	_____
Discount Store	_____

Step 2 When you visit each type of business, ask the manager to give you several ways that the stock turnover rate can be increased. Summarize your findings and share them with your classmates.

SECTION 6
CALCULATING INCOME AND LOSS IN MARKETING

Nearly everyone wants to earn money—to have an income. A business must also earn an *income* (profit) for the owner or owners. This section will explain what the terms *income* and *loss* mean and show how they are determined. Study the terminology, ideas, and sample problems presented. Complete the problems at the end of the section. Doing these problems correctly will show that you understand the basics of business income and loss.

After completing this section, you will be able to:

1. Explain what is meant by net income or loss.
2. Calculate net income or loss for a service business.
3. Calculate net income or loss for a merchandising business.
4. Calculate net income as a percentage of sales.
5. Construct an income statement for a merchandising business.

MEANING OF NET INCOME OR LOSS

Gross income is the total amount of money resulting from business activities (sales). *Net income* (profit) is the amount of money left after all the costs of operating the business have been paid. If operating costs are more than the amount of money taken in, a *net loss* is the result. People in business are very interested in this income or loss figure because it shows them whether their efforts have been profitable.

NET INCOME OR LOSS FOR A SERVICE BUSINESS

A business that sells services (instead of merchandise) is called a *service business*. Finding the net income or loss for this type of business is not difficult. To find whether a service business has made a net income or a net loss during a given period (usually one month or one year) you must know just two amounts:

1. Gross Income (sales from services provided)
2. Total Operating Expenses (costs of doing business)

Gross Income for Services Provided

All money received for services provided is the gross income (sales) for the period. For example, if Cache Recreation Rentals had equipment rentals of $20,000 for a year, this figure would represent their annual gross income (sales) for services provided.

1
Learning Activity

Mountain West Ski Resort had income from the following sources. Determine the gross income.

Downhill Ski Equipment Rentals	$28,000
Ski Lift Ticket Sales	$112,000
Snowmobile Rentals	$14,800
Cross Country Ski Equipment	$8,600
Gross Income (Sales)	$_____

Operating Expenses of Service Business

All costs of doing business are referred to as *operating expenses*. The usual operating expense items for a service business such as Cache Recreation Rentals might include:

1. *Salary Expense*—Wages paid to employees.
2. *Advertising Expense*—Money paid out for promotion in newspapers, radio, etc.
3. *Gasoline Expense*—Money paid out for gasoline for the operation of rental equipment.
4. *Repairs and Maintenance Expense*—Money paid out to keep rental equipment in operation.
5. *Rent Expense*—Money paid out for use of a building.

For a service business such as a tour guide company, all costs of doing business are called operating expenses.

6. *Utilities Expense*—Money paid out for heat, electricity, and telephone.
7. *Supplies Expense*—Money paid out for postage, office supplies, uniforms, etc.

If Cache Recreation Rentals had an annual salary expense of $10,500, advertising expense of $500, gasoline expense of $2,400, repairs and maintenance expense of $2,350, rent expense of $1,500, utilities expense of $400, and supplies expense of $350, the total expenses of operating the business for the year would be $18,000.

Cache Recreation Rentals

Operating Expenses

Salary Expense	$10,500
Advertising Expense	500
Gasoline Expense	2,400
Repairs and Maintenance Expense	2,350
Rent Expense	1,500
Utilities Expense	400
Supplies Expense	350
Total Operating Expenses	$18,000

2
Learning Activity

Jerry's Car Wash had the following operating expenses for the year. Find the total expenses.

Salary Expense	$12,500
Advertising Expense	2,400
Rent Expense	2,100
Insurance Expense	300
Supplies Expense	250
Utilities Expense	450
Total Operating Expenses	$_____

Determining Net Income or Loss for a Service Business

Net income or loss is determined by subtracting the total operating expenses from gross income (sales) for services provided. Cache Recreation Rentals had a $30,000 total annual gross income (sales) for services provided and $18,000 total operating expenses. The net income for this service business for the year would be $12,000.

Cache Recreation Rentals
Net Income (January 1-December 31)

Gross Income (Sales)	$30,000
Less: Total Operating Expenses	− 18,000
Net Income or Loss	$12,000 Income

3
Learning Activity

Jerry's Car Wash had a total gross income (sales) for the year of $25,000. Using the operating expenses determined in Learning Activity 2, calculate the net income or loss.

Gross Income (Sales) $ _____

Less: Total Operating Expenses   − $ _____

Net Income or Loss $ _____

4
Learning Activity

The Midwestern Appliance Repair Shop had a total gross income (sales) of $34,200 for the year. Operating expenses for the year totaled $34,000. Calculate the net income or loss.

Gross Income (Sales) $ _____

Less: Total Operating Expenses   − $ _____

Net Income or Loss $ _____

NET INCOME OR LOSS FOR A MERCHANDISING BUSINESS

More information is needed to determine the net income or loss for a merchandising business than for a service business. In order to find out whether this type of business has a net income or a net loss during a given period of time (usually one month or one year), four amounts must be known:

1. Gross and Net Sales
2. Cost of Merchandise Sold
3. Gross Margin on Sales
4. Total Operating Expenses

Net Sales of Merchandise

Gross sales is the total value of all merchandise sold by a business. *Sales returns* is the value of all merchandise returned to a business. *Net sales* is the total value of merchandise sold after sales returns have been subtracted. (Customers return merchandise to the seller for several reasons: defective merchandise; wrong color, size or style; and lack of need for the merchandise.) For example, if Import Auto Parts had gross sales of $71,000 for the year and returned merchandise from customers amounting to $1,000, net sales would be $70,000.

<u>**Import Auto Parts**</u>

<u>**Net Sales**</u>

Gross Sales	$71,000
Less: Sales Returns	− 1,000
Net Sales	$70,000

5
Learning Activity

The Bicycle Shop had gross sales of $73,500 and sales returns of $2,500. Calculate net sales.

Gross Sales $ _____

Less: Sales Returns   − $ _____

Net Sales $ _____

Cost of Merchandise Sold

In order to calculate the cost of merchandise sold, the following values must be known:

1. *Value of Beginning Merchandise Inventory*—The value of merchandise on hand at the beginning of the month or year.

2. *Value of Merchandise Purchased*—All new merchandise purchased during the month or year.

3. *Value of Ending Merchandise Inventory*—The value of merchandise on hand at the end of the month or year.

The total amount of purchases made during the month or year added to the beginning merchandise inventory equals the cost of merchandise available for sale. The cost of merchandise sold is then determined by subtracting the ending merchandise inventory from the cost of merchandise available for sale.

$$\text{Beginning Merchandise Inventory} + \text{Purchases} = \text{Cost of Merchandise Available for Sale}$$

$$\text{Cost of Merchandise Available for Sale} - \text{Ending Merchandise Inventory} = \text{Cost of Merchandise Sold}$$

For example, Import Auto Parts had a beginning inventory on January 1 of $6,000. During the year additional merchandise was purchased totaling $41,200. On December 31, the ending inventory was $5,200.

Import Auto Parts
Cost of Merchandise Sold

(Time period—January 1 to December 31)

Beginning Merchandise Inventory	$ 6,000
Plus: Purchases	+ 41,200
Cost of Merchandise Available for Sale	$47,200
Less: Ending Merchandise Inventory	− 5,200
Cost of Merchandise Sold	$42,000

6
Learning Activity

The Bicycle Shop had a beginning inventory on January 1 of $32,000. During the year additional merchandise was purchased totaling $20,000. On December 31, the ending inventory was $12,500. Find the cost of merchandise sold.

Beginning Merchandise Inventory	$_____
Plus: Purchases	+ $_____
Cost of Merchandise Available for Sale	$_____
Less: Ending Merchandise Inventory	− $_____
Cost of Merchandise Sold	$_____

Gross Margin

Gross margin is the difference between net sales and the cost of merchandise sold. Earlier we determined that the net sales for Import Auto Parts were $70,000. The cost of merchandise sold was $42,000. To determine gross margin, subtract the cost of good sold ($42,000) from the net sales ($70,000). The difference is a gross margin of $28,000.

Import Auto Parts
Gross Margin

Net Sales	$70,000
Less: Cost of Merchandise Sold	− 42,000
Gross Margin	$28,000

7
Learning Activity

Using the information from Learning Activities 5 and 6, calculate gross margin for The Bicycle Shop.

Net Sales	$_____
Less: Cost of Merchandise Sold	− $_____
Gross Margin	$_____

Determining the Gross Margin as a Percentage of Sales

Gross margin is usually expressed as a percentage of net sales. Net sales for Import Auto Parts were $70,000. The gross margin was $28,000. To determine the gross margin as a percentage of net sales, divide the gross margin ($28,000) by the net sales ($70,000).

Import Auto Parts

Gross Margin as Percentage of Sales

Gross Margin ÷ Net Sales = Gross Margin %

$$\text{GM \%} = \frac{\text{Gross Margin}}{\text{Net Sales}} = \frac{\$28,000}{\$70,000} = 0.40 = 40\%$$

8
Learning Activity

Using the information from Learning Activity 7, calculate the gross margin as a percentage of net sales for The Bicycle Shop.

Gross Margin as Percentage of Net Sales ___44.4%___

Operating Expenses of Merchandising Business

Remember, in a service business all costs of doing business are referred to as *operating expenses*. In a merchandising business, however, the cost of merchandise sold is *not* considered an operating expense. Typical operating expenses for a merchandising business are similar to those of a service business and might include:

1. Salary Expense
2. Rent Expense
3. Advertising Expense
4. Supplies Expense
5. Utilities Expense
6. Insurance Expense

To determine the total operating expenses, add all expense items together. For example, if Import Auto Parts had a salary expense for the year of $10,000, rent expense of $2,500, advertising expense of $1,200, supplies expense of $500, utilities expense of $800, and insurance expense of $500, their total operating expenses would be $15,500.

Import Auto Parts

Operating Expenses

Salary Expense	$10,000
Rent Expense	2,500
Advertising Expense	1,200
Supplies Expense	500
Utilities Expense	800
Insurance Expense	500
Total Operating Expenses	$15,500

Illus. 6-2

One operating expense for a merchandising business is the advertising expense.

9
Learning Activity

The Bicycle Shop had the following operating expenses. Calculate the total operating expenses.

Salary Expense	$8,600
Rent Expense	6,000
Advertising Expense	1,250
Utilities Expense	1,200
Supplies Expense	375
Insurance Expense	600
Total Operating Expenses	$ _____

Determining Net Income or Loss for a Merchandising Business

Once gross margin and total operating expenses have been determined, calculating the net income is easy. Net income is found by subtracting the total operating expenses from gross margin. In the case of Import Auto Parts, it was determined that gross margin was $28,000 and total operating expenses were $15,500. This means that Import Auto Parts had a net income of $12,500.

Import Auto Parts

Net Income

Gross Margin	$28,000
Less: Total Operating Expenses	− 15,500
Net Income or Loss	$12,500 Income

10
Learning Activity

Using the information from Learning Activities 7 and 9, calculate the net income or loss for The Bicycle Shop.

Gross Margin $ _____

Less: Total Operating Expenses − $ _____

Net Income or Loss $ _____

DETERMINING NET INCOME AS A PERCENTAGE OF SALES

Making a reasonable income is a goal common to all businesses. Businesspersons are concerned with the income/sales relationship. By calculating net income as a percentage of sales, the businessperson can compare the profitability of the business with other similar businesses. *Net income as a percentage of sales* is the amount of income made for every dollar's worth of merchandise sold or service provided during a given period of time.

Import Auto Parts, for example, had net sales for the year of $70,000 and a net income of $12,500. To determine net income as a percentage of sales, divide the net income of $12,500 by the net sales of $70,000. This results in an 18 percent net income for the year (rounded).

Import Auto Parts
Net Income as Percentage of Sales

Net Income ÷ Net Sales = Net Income %

$$\frac{\$12,500}{\$70,000} = 0.178 = 18\% \text{ (rounded)}$$

11
Learning Activity

Using the information from Learning Activities 5 and 10, calculate net income as a percentage of sales for The Bicycle Shop.

Net Income ÷ Net Sales = Net Income %

_____ ÷ _____ = _____

CONSTRUCTING AN INCOME STATEMENT

All of the information discussed in this section can be visually presented on what is called an income statement. The *income statement* (or *profit and loss statement*) shows the marketing businessperson, in detail, how much money was made by the business over a period of time, usually a year. The following income statement details how Import Auto Parts made and spent money for the year.

Import Auto Parts
Income Statement

Gross Sales	$71,000	
Less: Sales Returns	− 1,000	
Net Sales		$70,000
Cost of Merchandise Sold:		
Beginning Merchandise Inventory	$ 6,000	
Plus: Purchases	+ 41,200	
Cost of Merchandise Available for Sale	47,200	
Less: Ending Inventory	− 5,200	
Less: Cost of Merchandise Sold		− 42,000
Gross Margin		$28,000
Operating Expenses:		
Salary Expense	$10,000	
Rent Expense	2,500	
Advertising Expense	1,200	
Supplies Expense	500	
Utilities Expense	800	
Insurance Expense	500	
Less: Total Operating Expenses		− 15,500
Net Income or Loss		$12,500

12
Learning Activity

Using the information from Learning Activities 5, 6, 7, 9, and 10, construct an income statement for The Bicycle Shop in the space below.

SECTION 6
USING MATH IN MARKETING

1. Explain why an understanding of income and loss is important to the businessperson.

to see profit

Effort

2. Viewmount Food Catering Service had a gross income (sales) of $18,800 for the month of April. Their expenses for the month were:

Salary Expense	$6,000
Cost of Food	8,400
Rent Expense	2,400
Utilities Expense	1,200
Depreciation Expense	1,000
Advertising Expense	800

   a. What were the total operating expenses for the month? $_____

   b. How much was the net income or loss for the month? $_____

3. Identify two ways that Viewmount Food Catering Service might increase their net income or eliminate their loss.

   a. _____

   b. _____

4. Total annual sales for the Sunnyside Sports Center were $972,000. Customers returned $7,200 worth of merchandise to the Sports Center during the year. What were the net sales for the year?

   $_____

5. Pants West, Inc., had total sales for the year of $542,000, sales returns of $14,000, a beginning inventory of $68,500, purchases throughout the year of $34,400, and an ending inventory of $68,100.

   a. What were net sales for the year? $_____

   b. What was the cost of the merchandise that was sold? $_____

   c. What was the gross margin? $_____

6. The Cottonwood Ski Shop had purchases of $15,800, total sales of $53,900, sales returns of $800, an ending inventory of $13,200, and a beginning inventory of $20,600.

   a. What were the net sales for the year? $_____

   b. What was the cost of the merchandise that was sold? $_____

   c. What was the gross margin? $_____

   d. What percentage of sales did the gross margin represent?   _____ %

7. The Cottonwood Ski Shop had a salary expense for the year of $12,500, rent expense of $2,300, insurance expense of $500, advertising expense of $2,050, and miscellaneous expenses of $800. (Use the information in Problem 6 when necessary.)

   a. What were the total operating expenses for the year? $_____

   b. What was the net income or loss? $_____

   c. What percentage of sales did the net income represent (round to the nearest hundredth percent)?   _____ %

Name _____

8. Calculate net income as a percentage of sales. (Round to the nearest tenth percent.)

	Sales	Net Income	Net Income as Percentage of Sales
a.	$313,477	$31,699	_____ %
b.	$795,000	$93,500	_____ %
c.	$42,750	$4,291	_____ %
d.	$1,765,400	$41,232	_____ %

9. For the following businesses, calculate the dollar amount of net income.

	Sales	Net Income as Percentage of Sales	Net Income
a.	$67,850	16.0%	$_____
b.	$1,376,500	3.4%	$_____
c.	$185,300	17.6%	$_____
d.	$276,470	7.5%	$_____

10. Neil's Auto Sound had total annual sales of $63,200, sales returns of $1,000, a beginning inventory of $5,800, purchases throughout the year of $45,500, and an ending inventory of $8,560. Expenses for the year were: salaries expense, $10,500; rent expense, $4,800; insurance expense, $380; advertising expense, $1,656; and miscellaneous expense, $439.

a. What were net sales for the year? $_____

b. What was the cost of merchandise that was sold? $_____

c. What was the gross margin? $_____

d. What percentage of sales did the gross margin represent? _____ %

e. What were the total operating expenses for the year? $_____

f. What was the net income or loss? $_____

g. What percentage of sales did the net income represent? _____ %

11. Using the information from Problem 10, construct an income statement for Neil's Auto Sound in the space below.

Gross Sales   42,000

    Sales Ret   1,020

             Net Sales 42,020   42,020

Cost of Merchandise

    B. I   5,000

    Purchases   45,500

                 51,300

    End I   8,560

Cost of Merd.   42,740

                17,460

               –17,775

Net In   1685.

SECTION 6
PROJECTS

6-1 PROJECT GOAL: To improve your understanding of income and loss.

Step 1 Interview three students who are not in your class to learn their views regarding the average net income of the businesses identified below. Record the estimated percentages in the spaces provided.

Type of Business	Student 1 Estimated Net Income Percentage	Student 2 Estimated Net Income Percentage	Student 3 Estimated Net Income Percentage
Appliance Store	_____	_____	_____
Apparel Store	_____	_____	_____
Automotive Parts Store	_____	_____	_____
Department Store	_____	_____	_____
Furniture Store	_____	_____	_____
Jewelry Store	_____	_____	_____
Supermarket	_____	_____	_____

Step 2 Compare the information gathered in Step 1 with the information given below. Are there differences? If so, why do you think these differences exist.

Type of Business*	Estimated Sales Volume	Estimated Average Net Income Percentage
Appliance Store	$250,000-$500,000	3.4%
Apparel Store	$25,000-$50,000	15.6%
Automotive Parts Store	$100,000-$150,000	7.3%
Department Store	$2-$5 million	4.2%
Furniture Store	$250,000-$500,000	5.9%
Jewelry Store	$100,000-$300,000	8.2%
Supermarket	(not available)	1.7%

Source: *Merchandising and Operating Results of Department Stores for 1977* (New York: National Retail Merchants Association, 1978).

*Industry-wide estimates of the average net income made on each of the different types of businesses.

6-2 PROJECT GOAL: To understand what the beginning worker can do to help raise net income.

Step 1 Interview an owner or manager of a merchandising or service business in your community. Find out different ways that the beginning worker can assist in improving the net income of a business. Record the suggestions in the space provided.

Suggestion 1:

Suggestion 2:

Suggestion 3:

Step 2 Compare the suggestions you receive with those of others in your class. Be prepared to discuss these suggestions in class.

INDEX